The 50 Greatest Love Letters of All Time

The 50 Greatest Love Letters of All Time

by David H. Lowenherz

A BYRON PREISS BOOK

Crown Publishers
New York

Copyright © 2002 by Byron Preiss Visual Publications Inc.
and Lion Heart Autographs, Inc.

Published by Crown Publishers, New York, New York.
Member of the Crown Publishing Group.

Random House, Inc. New York, Toronto, London, Sydney, Auckland
www.randomhouse.com

CROWN is a trademark and the Crown colophon
is a registered trademark of Random House, Inc.

Printed in the United States of America

Design by Mike Rivilis

Library of Congress Cataloging-in-Publication Data
The 50 greatest love letters of all time / [selected] by David H. Lowenherz—1st ed.
    "A Byron Preiss book."
    (hardcover)
    1. Love-letters. I. The fifty greatest love letters of all time. II. Lowenherz, David H.

PN6140.L7 A15 2002
808.83'3543—dc21   2001037115

ISBN 0-8129-3277-3

10 9 8 7 6 5 4

For my wife and son,
whose love lights the way.
—D.H.L.

A Note to the Reader

The letters reprinted in this collection are the most authentic and definitive versions available. To preserve the intimate and original nature of these letters, we made a conscious decision to reproduce them as they were first written, complete with spelling errors, grammatical imperfections, and, in some cases, antiquated terminology. We feel that these characteristics add to the charm and character of the letters. Besides, in the heat of impassioned expression, who has time for dictionaries?

Contents

Passionate Prose

Painful Separations

Fire and Ice

Forbidden Love

Introduction

GOING to him! Happy letter! Tell him —
Tell him the page I didn't write;
Tell him I only said the syntax,
And left the verb and the pronoun out.
Tell him just how the fingers hurried,
Then how they waded, slow, slow, slow;
And then you wished you had eyes in your pages,
So you could see what moved them so.

Tell him it wasn't a practised writer,
You guessed, from the way the sentence toiled;
You could hear the bodice tug, behind you,
As if it held but the might of a child;
You almost pitied it, you, it worked so.

from *Complete Poems* (1924) by Emily Dickinson

Sometimes nothing speaks louder than a silent word written on a piece of paper. With the recent advent of instant messaging and e-mail, the art of epistolary romance has made something of a comeback, albeit in the rather sterile environment of cyberspace — no handmade paper or fine penmanship here, and certainly no possibility of inhaling the fragrance of perfumed stationery!

The act of writing, however, gives us a chance to reflect in private before exposing our heart. The letters in this collection were selected not for their effusive display of affection, but for the authentic and broad range of feelings their authors reveal. Much the way light displays all the colors when broken by a prism, love expresses the spectrum of our emotions, and these letters offer a colorful glimpse into the soul of the writer.

Each letter reflects a theme or variation on the subject of love and, in doing so, provides a comprehensive definition of the word. You will read about passion, longing, despair, loss, anger, sadness, bitterness, sympathy, respect, friendship, gratitude, jealousy, doubt, and happiness. In fact, the entire range of human emotions is found in these missives.

As a dealer in rare letters and manuscripts for more than twenty years, I have been particularly fortunate to offer for sale some of the letters included in this collection, including Chagall, Hemingway, Rodgers, Sand, and Wright.

For obvious reasons, love letters rarely appear on the market—their personal nature makes them prone to destruction or to being locked away in private archives. Understandably, most people (particularly those in the public eye) prefer to keep the record of their intensely personal feelings confidential. Once sufficient time has passed, friends or relatives of the recipient sometimes give away or sell these treasured mementos. But these opportunities are infrequent.

The Hemingway letter included in this collection is just one of nearly thirty extraordinary letters written to Mary Welsh, Hemingway's last wife. They were found in a suitcase in Mary's apartment after her death, part of a larger collection of literary manuscripts and other material, including Hemingway's tax records and a list of drugs he was using to treat depression at the end of his life. They stand out as some of the most dramatic and revealing letters I've ever read. I had the indescribable pleasure of actually holding the original document in my hands.

After years of acquiring and selling rare documents and hundreds of hours of research, you now hold in your hands a collection of some of the greatest and most unusual love letters publicly available. I have included revealing correspondences between famous couples, among them, Admiral Nelson and Lady Hamilton, Zelda and F. Scott Fitzgerald, Frida Kahlo and Diego Rivera. I have also included writers as famous as Beethoven or as little known as Marjorie Fossa, a diehard Elvis fan. I wanted this collection to offer a diverse, unusual, and not always romantic view of love—love as it is lived, not only dreamed: passionate, possessed, and faithful, or cold, distant, and deceitful.

Some letters reveal an aspect of affection not limited to an exchange between lovers. For example, the two letters by Elizabeth and Robert Browning are not written to each other, but to Elizabeth's brother, George. They are exceptionally moving documents that underscore the deep love these two outstanding nineteenth-century poets felt toward each other, but chose to communicate to a third party.

One of the most poignant love letters in this collection is associated with a sensational trial of the nineteenth-century, that of Alfred Dreyfus. Unjustly accused, tried, and convicted of espionage, this French captain was framed by his fellow officers and deported for life to Devil's Island. The astonishing details of his case are too complicated to outline here, but the correspondence between Alfred Dreyfus and his wife,

Lucie, is a testament to their undying love and faith in each other throughout their ordeal. Captain Dreyfus was determined, at all costs, to defend his honor, clear his name, and do it all for the love and respect of his wife and two young children. But, with her husband isolated on a small island in the Atlantic, it was up to Lucie to fight to overturn an unjust verdict founded on institutionalized anti-Semitism. Her ultimate success not only underscores her tenacity and courage, but her willingness, in the name of love, to rescue the honor and life of her beloved husband. So while Alfred's letter to Lucie is quite touching, the circumstances surrounding it make the contents even more so.

As our culture speeds incessantly toward faster and more convenient forms of communication, there is still something powerful in patiently scripted words, as they languorously flow onto a sheet of paper. You find yourself asking, How long did it take to choose the right word to convey the right tone and evoke the right feeling that will result, one hopes, in the right response? Was it a slow, laborious affair or a quick scribble? Coffee cup rings, tearstains, cross-outs, or smeared ink all contribute clues to the writer's state of mind.

As you read through the following letters, I hope you will not only become immersed in the feelings of those who wrote them, but will also speculate on what the recipients must have felt when they tore open the envelope and breathlessly, or anxiously, read the contents.

Tender Love

Horatio Nelson to Emma Hamilton

"I love you most tenderly and affectionately . . ."

Horatio Nelson (1758–1805). British admiral. Nelson, whose naval career began when he was twelve, advanced to the rank of commodore in 1796. A year later, he helped the British defeat the Spanish, French, and Dutch fleets at Cape St. Vincent and was promoted to rear admiral. That same year, he was shot in the right elbow, suffered through a botched amputation, and returned to active duty a few months later. In 1798, after his victory over the French at Abu Qir Bay (the Battle of the Nile), Nelson renewed his acquaintance with the extremely beautiful and vivacious Lady Emma Hamilton (nee Lyon; 1765–1815)who was the wife of the scholar and diplomat Sir William Hamilton. Emma had helped arrange a hero's welcome for Nelson when he returned to port in Naples, Italy, where her husband was the British envoy. Their liaison

"I hope to have letters from you who I hold dearer than any other person in this World..."

Emma Hamilton

Horatio Viscount Nelson

soon resulted in the birth of a daughter, Horatia, in 1801. On Nelson's instructions, Emma purchased a country house, Merton Place, in Surrey, outside London, and it was here that Nelson, as he writes below, was to spend many happy days. Sir William, now best remembered for tolerating their affair, died April 6, 1803, with his wife and her lover at his side. This letter, written on board the Victory *from October 11 to the 13, is one of the very last Nelson wrote to his beloved Emma, before his decisive victory over the French, and his death off Trafalgar on October 21, 1805.*

Mr. Denis request of Lt. Hargraves introduction shall be attended to but it must be considered that very few opportunities offer of ever getting on board the Commander-in-chief's ship in the Winter Months and, our battle I hope will be over long before the summer days. The wind has blown so fresh these two days that the Enemy if so disposed have not had the power of putting to Sea which I am firmly of opinion they intend. God send it for our selves as well as that of our Country well over. Our friend Sutton is going home for his health. Hoste has Amphion and Sir Wm Bolton Eurydice which I hope the Admiralty will approve. This is the last chance of Sir Billys making a fortune if he is active and persevering he may do it and be easy for life. Oh my Beloved Emma how I envy Sutton going home, his going to Merton and seeing you and Horatia. I do really feel that the 25 days I was at Merton was the very happiest of my life. Would to God they were to be passed over again but that time will I trust soon come and many many more days added to them. I have been as you may believe made very uneasy or rather uncomfortable by the situation of Sir Robt. Calder. He was to have gone home in another ship . . . However

I have given way to his misery and have directed the Prince of Wales to carry him to Spithead for whatever the result of the enquiry might be. I think he has a right to be treated with Respect, therefore My Dear Emma do not form any opinion abt. him till the trial is over. I am working like a horse in a Mill but never the nearer finishing my task which I find difficulty enough in keeping clear from confusion but I never allow it to accumulate. Agamemnon is in sight and I hope to have letters from you who I hold dearer than any other person in this World and I shall hope to hear that all our family goes on well at that dear dear Cottage. Believe all I would say upon this occasion but letters being in quarantine may be read, not that I care who knows that I love you most tenderly and affectionately. I send you Adam Campbell's letter & copy of those from the King & Queen. You see they would never wish me out of the Mediterranean. Kiss Dear Horatia a thousand times for Your faithful Nelson & Bronte.

Though she inherited money from both her husband and Nelson, Emma squandered most of it and died, nearly destitute, in Calais, France. Horatia went on to marry an English clergyman and helped rear a large family.

George A. Custer to Elizabeth Custer

"Yours through time and eternity . . ."

George Armstrong Custer (1839–1876). American general. The son of a blacksmith who graduated last in his West Point class of 1861, George went on to become a Civil War cavalry commander. Although eleven horses were shot out from under him, he was wounded only once, and was promoted to brigadier general at the age of twenty-three, and major general at twenty-five. In 1866, George became a lieutenant colonel of the 7th Cavalry, and took part in General Winfield Scott Hancock's expedition against the Plains Indians. His wife, Elizabeth (nee Bacon), or "Libbie," the daughter of an Ohio judge, was a well-educated, strong-minded woman with an ambitious spirit. She initially refused to marry George until he promised never to drink, swear, or gamble again, most of which he steadfastly continued to do. Her devotion was legendary, as she followed him throughout his military campaigns, staying in tents,

George, here seen in uniform, is seated with Libbie, with his brother, Thomas, standing behind them.

farms, and boardinghouses. *His feelings toward her were no less devotional—in 1867, George was court-martialed and suspended for one year without pay for having made an unauthorized visit to his wife at a nearby fort. On June 25, 1876, in an attempt to drive the Sioux and Cheyenne Indian tribes off Montana land, George, his brother Thomas, and 266 men under his command were massacred at the Battle of Little Bighorn.*

The following letter was written shortly after the battle of Yellow Tavern, near Richmond, Virginia (May 11, 1864), an engagement in which George participated, and where the great Confederate general James Ewell Brown, or "JEB," Stuart was mortally wounded.

"With thoughts of my darling...my last prayer will be for her, my last breath will speak her name..."

Dear little "durl"—Again I am called on to bid you adieu for a short period. To-morrow morning two Divisions, 1st and 2nd, of this Corps set out on another raid. We may be gone two or three weeks. I will write, the first opportunity. Keep up a stout heart, and remember the successful issue of the past. God and success have hitherto attended us. May we not hope for a continuance of His blessing?

With thoughts of my darling and with the holy inspiration of a just and noble cause I gladly set out to discharge my duty to my country with a willing heart. Need I repeat to my darling that while living she is my all, and if Destiny wills me to die, wills that my country needs my death, my last prayer will be for her, my last breath will speak her name and that Heaven will not be Heaven till we are joined together. Write to Monroe and tell them of my absence.

Yours through time and eternity,
Autie

John Ruskin to Euphemia Ruskin

". . . to think of all my happy hours . . ."

John Ruskin (1819–1900). English writer and art critic whose scholar-ship and opinions had considerable influence on Victorian English taste. John's parents recognized their son's complex genius from an early age, and tended to shelter him from the world. Their protection, however, could not help John overcome an unrequited love affair at the age of seventeen, which set the stage for his future relationships. High strung and self-centered, he cautiously entered into an engagement with Euphemia ("Effie") Gray, the Scottish daughter of family friends, and the two were married in April 1848. Though few of their love letters survive, many were written, and some were quite passionate. Nevertheless, their marriage seems never to have been consummated. John wanted to be surrounded by art and artists, and one of his close friendships was with the English painter John Everett Millais, with whom Effie fell in love. As soon as

Millais was elected to the Royal Academy—an election which assured him of commissions and a financially secure future—Effie left John, obtained an annulment in July 1854, and married Millais several months later. Together they had eight children. John's father once slyly observed that "Effie is much better calculated for society than he [John] is—He is best in print." This letter from John to Effie dates from June 1849.

I have been thinking of you a great deal in my walks today, as of course I always do when I am not busy, but when I am measuring or drawing mountains, I forget myself—and my wife both; if I did not I could not stop so long away from her; for I begin to wonder whether I am married at all—and to think of all my happy hours, and soft slumber in my dearest lady's arms, as a dream—However I feel—in such cases—for my last letter and look at the signature and see that it is all right. I got one on Friday; that in which you tell me you are better—thank God; and that your father is so much happier, and that Alice is so winning and that you would like a little Alice of our own, so should I; a little Effie, at least. Only I wish they weren't so small at first that one hardly knows what one has got hold of . . .

I have for seven years thought over the various topics of dissuasion which you mention—nor have I yet come to any conclusion—but I asked you for your own feelings, as their expression would in some sort turn the scale with me—not affirmatively indeed—but negatively: as, if you were to tell me that you would be unhappy, living in Switzerland, I should dismiss the subject from my mind; while if you told me you could be comfortable there, I should retain the thought for future consideration, as circumstances may turn out. I wanted therefore to know, not so much whether you would like places of which you can at present form no conception, as whether you had any plans or visions of your own respecting this matter— any castles in the air which I could realize—or any yearnings which I could supply. I myself have for some time wished to have a home proper, where I could alter a room without asking leave—and without taking leave of it after it was altered . . .

Poor Venice—I saw they were bombarding it last week. How all my visions about taking you there; and bringing you here, have been destroyed: Well, it might have been too much happiness to be good for me; as it would certainly have been more than I deserved—I mean in the common human sense, —since all our happiness is actually more than we deserve. I reconcile myself to your absence only by baking myself in the Sun, and thinking 'Effie couldn't have stood this' . . .

It is a lovely morning with broken clouds and one [paper torn] the great snow precipices of Mont Blanc—itself as high as [paper torn] cliffs of Dover, thought merely in the thickness of the snow, shows through a gap in the cloud like what one might fancy a piece of the moon, if one could break it up when it was new: there are such lovely snow lines beside it, too, white and waving—I don't know what they are like in the world, unless it be my Effie's shoulders . . .

Wolfgang Amadeus Mozart to Constanze Mozart

"Good night, little mouse"

Wolfgang Amadeus Mozart (1756–1791). Austrian composer of more than 600 works, many of which are among the greatest instrumental and vocal creations of Western civilization. When just six years old, Mozart toured throughout Europe as a pianist with his father Leopold. By 1780, he had fallen in love with Aloysia Weber, the daughter of a copyist. When Aloysia married a court actor, Mozart's affections shifted to her younger sister, Constanze. In December 1781, he notified his father of his intentions to marry her, but it is unlikely that his father approved, for any letters that revealed the elder Mozart's reactions were later destroyed by Constanze. Mozart and Constanze were married on August 4, 1782, in the magnificent St. Stephen's Cathedral in Vienna, and by all accounts had a happy marriage. Tragically, of their six children, only two survived into adulthood. In 1789, Mozart accompanied

Prince Karl Lichnowsky on a trip through Germany, visiting that country's leading musical centers: Berlin, Leipzig, and Dresden, from where this letter—one of eleven written during the trip—was sent on April 13, 1789.

We expected to reach Dresden after dinner on Saturday, but we did not arrive until yesterday, Sunday, at two o'clock in the afternoon, because the roads were so bad. All the same I went yesterday to the Neumanns, where Madame Duschek is staying, in order to deliver her husband's letter. Her room is on the third floor beside the corridor and from it you can see anyone who is coming to the house. When I arrived at the door, Herr Neumann was already there and asked me to whom he had the honor to speak. "That I shall tell you in a moment," I replied, "but please be so kind as to call Madame Duschek, so that my joke may not be spoilt." But at the same moment Madame Duschek stood before me for she had recognized me from the window and had said at once: "Why here comes someone who is very like Mozart." Well, we were all delighted. There was a large party, consisting entirely of ugly women, who by their charm, however, made up for their lack of beauty. The Prince and I are going to breakfast there today; we shall then see Neumann and then the chapel. Tomorrow or the day after we shall leave for Leipzig. All the Neumanns and the Duscheks send their greetings to you and also to my brother-in-law Lange and his wife. Dearest little wife, if only I had a letter from you! If I were to tell you all the things I do with your dear portrait, I think that you would often laugh. For instance, when I take it out of its case, I say, "Good-day, Stanzerl!—Good-day, little rascal, pussy-pussy, little turned-up nose, little bagatelle,

"Dearest little wife, if only I had a letter from you! ...

Today is the sixth day since I left you and by Heaven, it seems a year."

Schluck and Druck," and when I put it away again, I let it slip in very slowly, saying all the time, "Stu-Stu-Stu-Stu!" with the peculiar emphasis which this word so full of meaning demands, and then just at the last, quickly, "Good night, little mouse, sleep well." Well, I suppose I have been writing something very foolish (to the world at all events); but to us who love each other so dearly, it is not foolish at all. Today is the sixth day since I left you and by Heaven, it seems a year. I expect you will have some difficulty here and there in reading my letter, because I am writing in a hurry and therefore rather badly.

Adieu, my only love! The carriage is waiting. This time I do not say: "Hurrah—the carriage has come at last," but "male." [Maledetto?] Farewell, and love me forever as I love you. I kiss you a million times most lovingly and am ever your husband who loves you tenderly.

PS—How is our Karl behaving? Well, I hope. Kiss him for me . . . Remember, you must not regulate the length of your letters by that of mine. Mine are rather short, but only because I am in a hurry. If I were not, I should cover a whole sheet. But you have more leisure. Adieu.

Elizabeth Barrett Browning
to George Barrett

"... he loved me with no ordinary affection."

Elizabeth Barrett Browning (1806–1861). English poet and wife of Robert Browning. The eldest of twelve children, Elizabeth was part Creole, and her family had lived in Jamaica for centuries. Born and bred in England, young Elizabeth became seriously ill at the age of fifteen, and remained an invalid for the rest of her life, dependent on morphine to ease her pain. Broken by the death of one of her brothers and the tyrannical rule of her father, Elizabeth became a recluse in her bedroom on Wimpole Street, London, for five years. In 1844, she published a book of poetry that captured the attention of Robert Browning (1812–1889), who sent her a telegram of appreciation. Over the course of the next twenty months, they exchanged nearly 600 letters, but her father remained bitterly opposed to their relationship (or the marriage of any of his children). Elizabeth and Robert secretly married on September 12, 1846. This exceptionally moving letter to her brother, George, was posted just before she and Robert left for Italy. Her father never spoke to her again.

I throw myself on your affection for me and beseech of God that it may hold under the weight—dearest George, Go to your room & read this letter—and I entreat you by all that we both hold dearest, to hold me still dear after the communication which it remains to me to make to yourself and to leave you in order to be communicated to others in the way that shall seem best to your judgement. And Oh, love me George, while you are reading it. Love me—that I may find pardon in your heart after it is read.

Mr. Browning has been attached to me for nearly two years—At first and for long I could not believe that he (who is what you know a little) could care for such as I, except in an illusion and a dream. I put an end (as I thought) briefly to the subject. I felt certain that a few days & a little more light on my ghastly face, would lead him to thank me for my negative, and I bade him not to observe that if my position had not been exceptional, I should not have received him at all. With a protest, he submitted, and months passed on so. Still he came continually & wrote & made me feel (though observing my conditions in the form) made me feel with every breath I drew in his presence, that he loved me with no ordinary affection. But I believed that it would be a wrong to such a man, to cast on him the burden of my sickly life, & to ruin him by his own generosity—He was too good for me, I knew, but I tried to be as generous. I showed him that I was altogether bruised and broken—that setting aside my health which, however improved, was liable to fail with every withdrawing of the sun—that the common advantages of youth & good spirits had gone from me & that I was an undone creature for the pleasures of life, as for its social duties.

His answer was—not the common gallantries which come so easily to the lips of men—but simply that he loved me—he met argument with fact. He told me—that with himself also, the early freshness of youth had gone by, & that throughout it he had not been able to love any woman—that he loved now for the first time & the last. That, as to the question of my health, he had been under the impression when he first declared his attachment to me, that I was suffering from an incurable injury on the spine, which would prevent my ever standing up before his eyes. If that had been true—he bade tell me how it should have operated in suppressing any pure attachment of a soul to a soul. For his part, he had desired under those circumstances, to attain to the right of sitting by my sofa just two hours in the day as one of my brothers might—and he preferred, of deliberate choice, the realization of such a dream, to the highest, which should exclude me, in the world—But he would not, he said, torment me—He would wait, if I pleased, twenty years, till we both should grow old, & then at the latest,—too late,—I should understand him as he understood himself right now—& should know that he loved me with ineffaceable love. In the meanwhile, what he asked I had it in my power to give. He did not ask me to dance or sing,—but to help him to work and to live—to live a useful life & to die a happy death—that was in my power.

And this was the attachment, George, I have had to do with, & this man—Such a man.—Noble he is—his intellect the least of his gifts! His love showed itself to me like a vocation. And I a mere woman, feeling as a woman must, & in circumstances which made every proof of devotion sink down to the deepest of my heart where the deep sorrow was before. Did he not come in my adversity? When I had done with life, did he not come to me. Call to mind the sorrow & the solitude, & how, in these long years, the feeling of personal vanity had died out of me, till I was grateful to all those who a little could bear with me personally. And he, such a man! Why men have talked to me before of what they called love—but never for any one, could I think even, of relinquishing the single life with which I was contented. I never believed that a man whom I could love (I hated having a need to look up high in order to love) . . . could be satisfied with loving me. And yet he did—does. Then we have one mind on all subjects—& the solemner they are, the nearer we seem to approach. If poets, we are together, still more we are Christians. For these nearly two years we have known each other's opinions & thoughts & feelings, weakness & strength, as few persons in the position have had equal opportunities of doing. And knowing me perfectly he has entirely loved me—At last, I only could say—"Wait till the winter—You will see that I shall be ill again—If not, I will leave it to you." I believed I should be ill again certainly. But the winter came, mild & wonderful—I did not fail in health—nor to him.

I beseech you, George, to judge me gently, looking to the peculiar circumstances—& above all, to acquit him wholly. I claim the whole responsibility of his omission of the usual application to my father & friends—for he was about to do it—anxious to do it—& I stopped him. That blame therefore belongs to me. But I knew, & you know, what the consequence of that application would have been—we should have been separated from that moment. He is not rich—which would have been an obstacle—At any rate, I could not physically bear to encounter agitating opposition from those I tenderly loved—& to act openly in defiance of Papa's will, would have been more impossible for me than to use the right which I believe to be mine, of taking a step so strictly personal, on my own responsibility. We both of us comprehend life in a simpler way than generally is done, and to live happily according to our conscience, we do not need to be richer than we are. I do beseech you, George, to look

"Love me—that I may find pardon in your heart after it is read."

to the circumstances & judge me gently, & see that, having resolved to give my life to one who is in my eyes the noblest of all men & who loves me as such a man can love—there was no way possible to my weakness but the way adopted with this pain. The motives are altogether different from any supposable want of respect & affection where I owe them most tenderly. I beseech you to understand this—I beseech you to lay it before my dearest papa, that it is so—Also, to have consulted one of you, would have been ungenerous & have involved you in my blame I have therefore consulted not one of you. I here declare that everyone in the house is absolutely ignorant & innocent of all participation in this act of my own. I love you too dearly, too tenderly, to have done you such injustice. Forgive me all of you for the act itself, for the sake of the love which came before it—& follows after it—for never (whether you pardon or reproach me) will an hour pass during my absence from you, in which I shall not think of you with tenderest thoughts . . .

And I think it due to myself, to observe, that I have seen Mr. Browning only in this house & openly—except the day of our meeting in the church of this parish in order to becoming his wife in the presence of the two necessary witnesses. We go across France, down the Seine & Rhone to Pisa for the winter, in submission to the conditions considered necessary for the re-establishment of my health, & shall return in the next summer. As soon as he became aware that I had the little money which is mine, he wished much that I would leave it to my sisters, & go to him penniless—But this, which I would have acceded to under ordinary circumstances, I resisted on the ground of my health—the uncertainty of which seemed to make it a duty to me to keep from being a burden to him—at least in a pecuniary respect.

George, dear George, read the enclosed letter for my dearest Papa, & then—breaking gently the news of it—give it to him to read. Also if he would deign to read this letter addressed to you—I should be grateful—I wish him in justice, & beseech him in affection, to understand the whole bearings of this case. George, believe of me, that I have endeavoured in all this matter to do right according to my own view of rights & right-eousness—If it is not your view, bear with me & pardon me. Do you all pardon me, my beloved ones, & believe that if I could have benefitted any of you by staying here, I would have stayed. Have I not done for you what I could, always? When I could—Now I am weak. And if in this crisis I were to do otherwise that what I am about to do, there would be a victim without an expiation, & a sacrifice without an object. My spirits would have festered on in this enforced prison, & none of you all would have been the happier for what would have [been] bitter to me. Also, I should have wronged another. I cannot do it.

If you have any affection for me, George, dearest George, let me hear a word—at Orleans—let me hear. I will write—I bless you, I love you—

Michelangelo Buonarroti
to Vittoria Colonna

"... he who loves does not sleep ..."

Michelangelo Buonarroti (1475–1564). One of the most important artists of the Italian High Renaissance. Known primarily as a painter, sculptor, and architect, he was also an accomplished poet, who authored several hundred sonnets and madrigals. In 1538, he met the poet Vittoria Colonna (1492–1547), and they corresponded regularly, exchanging philosophical letters and poems. A homosexual, Michelangelo's relationship with the significantly younger marchioness was purely platonic. He was at her bedside when she died, and wrote in commemoration, "Nature, that never made so fair a face, remained ashamed, and tears were in all eyes."

Lady Marchioness: Since I am in Rome, I do not feel that the Crucifix should be left to Master Tommaso and he should be made the go-between between your ladyship and me your servant, so that I can do you a service, and especially since I have wished to do more for you than for any man I ever knew in the world; but the great busyness in which I have been and am has not allowed me to let your ladyship know this, and since I know you know that love wants no master, and that he who loves does not sleep, go-betweens were still less suitable; and though it might seem I did not remember, I was doing something I did not speak of, in order to effect something you did not expect. My plan has been ruined: "Who soon forgets such trust does evilly."

Your ladyship's servant
Michelangelo Buonarroti in Rome

Harry Truman to Bess Wallace

"I'm sure crazy to see you."

Harry Truman (1884–1972). Thirty-third president of the United States, and considered by many to be one of America's greatest leaders. When the United States entered World War I in April 1917, Harry, despite his age (thirty-three) and two previous tours in the National Guard (1905–1919), volunteered in June. As this letter shows, he was eager to fight not only for his country, but for France as well. Harry was captain of Battery D, a field artillery unit that saw action throughout France, including the Battle of Argonne in 1918, firing its last shot fifteen minutes before the armistice was declared at 11 A.M. on November 11, 1918. He was greatly admired by the soldiers and officers serving under his command. Harry, who had begun courting his childhood friend, Elizabeth "Bess" Wallace, in 1910, married her two months after his return to the United States in June 1919.

This letter was written from France on May 5, 1918, to his future wife, Bess, whom he would often affectionately refer to as "The Boss."

Harry Truman

Dear Bess,

We work so hard during the week we don't have time to think of anything but work. Sundays are sure dull though if we don't get letters to read.

Be sure and write and keep writing and I'll do the same. We sure appreciate letters and more letters from home. France is France and a grand place for Frenchmen. I don't

"French girls are pretty and chic but they cannot hold a candle to American girls."

Bess Truman

blame them for fighting for it and I'm for helping them, but give me America, Missouri, and Jackson County for mine with the finest girl in the world at the county seat. French girls are pretty and chic but they cannot hold a candle to American girls. Every man in this room agrees with me too. It's raining today for a change after starting out with a grand sunrise and a fine morning. We've seen the sun about four days since we've been in France. The weather doesn't bother us much, but I'll bet a Frenchman would suffocate if he got into a heated room. They're never warm from September to June. They thrive on it though. Be sure and write to me much and often, for I can always put in another week happily if I get at least one letter. The more, the better. I'm sure crazy to see you.

George Bush to
Barbara Pierce

". . . to know that you love me means my life."

George Herbert Walker Bush (b. 1924). Forty-first president of the United States; son of Senator Prescott Bush and father of Governor Jeb Bush of Florida and America's forty-third president, George W. Bush. The U.S. Navy's youngest pilot during World War II, he completed fifty-eight combat missions and was awarded the Distinguished Flying Cross. He met his future wife, Barbara Pierce, at a Christmas dance during her junior year at Ashley Hall in South Carolina. George was then a senior at Phillips Academy in Andover, Massachusetts. Prior to his World War II service, the two were engaged, and he married her while home on leave in January 1945. Barbara lost all of George's letters from the war, except the following, which was kept in her engagement scrapbook.

Dec. 12, 1943

My darling Bar,

This should be a very easy letter to write—words should come easily and in short it should be simple for me to tell you how desperately happy I was to open the paper and see the announcement of our engagement, but somehow I can't possibly say all in a letter I should like to.

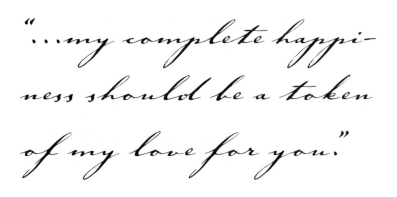

"...my complete happiness should be a token of my love for you."

I love you, precious, with all my heart and to know that you love me means my life. How often I have thought about the immeasurable joy that will be ours some day. How lucky our children will be to have a mother like you—

As the days go by the time of our departure draws nearer. For a long time I had anxiously looked forward to the day when we would go aboard and set to sea. It seemed that obtaining that goal would be all I could desire for some time, but, Bar, you have changed all that. I cannot say that I do not want to go—for that would be a lie. We have been working for a long time with a single purpose in mind, to be so equipped that we could meet and defeat our enemy. I do want to go because it is my part, but now leaving presents itself not as an adventure but as a job which I hope will be over before long. Even now, with a good while between us and the sea, I am thinking of getting back. This may sound melodramatic, but if it does it is only my inadequacy to say what I mean. Bar, you have made my life full of everything I could ever dream of—my complete happiness should be a token of my love for you.

Wednesday is definitely the commissioning and I do hope you'll be there. I'll call Mum tomorrow about my plan. A lot of fellows put down their parents or wives and they aren't going so you could pass as a Mrs.—Just say you lost the invite and give your name. They'll check the list and you'll be in. How proud I'll be if you can come.

George Bush

I'll tell you all about the latest flying developments later. We have so much to do and so little time to do it in. It is frightening at times. The seriousness of this thing is beginning to strike home. I have been made asst. gunnery officer and when Lt. Houle leaves I will be gunnery officer. I'm afraid I know very little about it but I am excited at having such a job. I'll tell you all about this later too.

The wind of late has been blowing like mad and our flying has been cut to a minimum. My plane, #2 now, is up at Quonset, having a camera installed. It is Bar #2 but purely in spirit since the Atlantic fleet won't let us have names on our planes.

Goodnite, my beautiful. Everytime I say beautiful you about kill me but you'll have to accept it—

I hope I get Thursday off—there's still a chance. All my love darling—

Poppy
public fiancé as of 12/12/43

Kahlil Gibran to Mary Haskell

"You are a life-giver, Mary."

Kahlil Gibran (1883–1931). Lebanese-American poet, artist, and philosopher best known for his short work, The Prophet *(1923), which, in America alone, has sold more than nine million copies. Born in Bsharri, Lebanon, he arrived in Boston at the age of twelve, and by twenty-one had already made a name for himself in the art world. The* Prophet *has as its hero Kahlil ("Almustafa") and his muse Mary Haskell ("Almitra"), Kahlil's patron and the recipient of the letter quoted here. His letters to Mary begin in 1908, and continue through to the year of his death at forty-eight in 1931. Though filled with warmth and sensuality, outside evidence suggests that their relationship remained platonic. Additionally, there is some controversy as to whether Kahlil, who was remarkably (and suspiciously) aware of his literary talent and personal charisma, may have initiated and maintained his relationship with the wealthy Mary for financial gain. Is this July 8, 1914, love letter written from the heart or the* porte-monnaie, *or both?*

You have the great gift of understanding, beloved Mary. You are a life-giver, Mary. You are like the Great Spirit, who befriends man not only to share his life, but to add to it. My knowing you is the greatest thing in my days and nights, a miracle quite outside the natural order of things.

I have always held, with my Madman, that those who understand us enslave something in us. It is not so with you. Your understanding of me is the most peaceful freedom I have known. And in the last two hours of your last visit you took my heart in your hand and found a black spot in it. But just as soon as you found the spot it was erased forever, and I became absolutely chainless.

And now you are a hermit in a mountain. To me nothing seems more delightful than to be a hermit in a place "full of beautiful hidden places." But please, beloved, do not take any risks. Being a hermit once will not satisfy your hungry soul, and you must keep well and strong in order to be a hermit again.

The laurel-leaves and balm-leaves are filling this place with the most enchanting fragrance. God bless you for sending them to me.

Love from Kahlil

Benjamin Franklin to Madame Brillon

". . . no other ears but mine be allowed to be charmed by those sweet sounds"

Benjamin Franklin (1706–1790). Author, printer, inventor, composer, patriot, diplomat, and statesman, Franklin was part of that unique circle of American Revolutionaries, including Thomas Paine, George Washington, and Thomas Jefferson, whose personalities and deeds forever made their mark on our country's history. Arriving in Paris in December 1776 as part of a three-man commission to obtain economic and military assistance from France at the outbreak of the American Revolution, Franklin soon became the darling of French society. Despite his seventy years, he was pursued by and a pursuer of several well-born ladies. One of them, Anne-Louise d'Hardancourt Brillon de Jouy, the wife of his neighbor, and the recipient of the letter below, was an accomplished musician who lovingly referred to the elder statesman as "Mon cher papa."

Franklin, eager to improve his French language abilities, wrote numerous letters to the lovely Madame Brillon (including several that admitted to sinfully coveting his neighbor's wife) who corrected and returned them to her ardent correspondent. Their intimacy, however, never seemed to go much beyond Madame sitting in Franklin's lap, imparting a few genteel kisses, and coquettishly refusing to give him what he incessantly made clear he desired. Nevertheless, when Madame Brillon found out that she was not the only object of his attention, she observed that although Franklin may have only one sin, "it has so many branches, it is repeated so often that it would take infinite calculations to assess its magnitude . . . The dangerous system you are forever trying to demonstrate, my dear papa, that the friendship a man has for women can be divided ad infinitum—this is something I shall never put up with." Franklin replied:

10 November 1779

What a difference, my dear friend, between you and me! You find innumerable faults in me, whereas I see only one fault in you (but perhaps it is the fault of my glasses). I mean this kind of avarice which leads you to seek a monopoly on all my affections, and not to allow me any for the agreeable ladies of your country. Do you imagine that it is impossible for my affection (or my tenderness) to be divided without being diminished? You deceive yourself, and you forget the playful manner with which you stopped me. You renounce and totally exclude all that might be of the flesh in our affection, allowing me only some kisses, civil and honest, such as you might grant your little cousins. What am I receiving that is so special as to prevent me from giving the same to others, without taking from what belongs to you? . . . The sweet sounds brought forth from the

"...I see only one fault in you...avarice which leads you to seek a monopoly on all my affections..."

pianoforte by your clever hands can be enjoyed by twenty people simultaneously without diminishing at all the pleasure you so obligingly mean for me, and I could, with as little reason, demand from your affection that no other ears but mine be allowed to be charmed by those sweet sounds.

Crazy
for
You

Jack London to Anna Strunsky

"You elude me. I cannot place you . . ."

Jack London (1876–1916). American novelist and short story writer. Born John Griffith Chaney in San Francisco, the illegitimate son of an astrologer, Jack lived with his mother, a spiritualist, and took the sur- name, London, from his stepfather. Jack's works, including The Call of the Wild *(1903),* The Sea Wolf *(1904), and* White Fang *(1905), depict a romanticized notion of survival. His own life was full of adventure: sailor, tramp, socialist, political candidate, and Yukon gold miner. By the time he was twenty-one, his life read like one of his beloved adventure stories. Returning to San Francisco from Alaska, his career flourished, and he wrote fifty books of fiction and nonfiction in seventeen years. In December 1899, Jack encountered Anna Strunsky at a meeting of the Socialist Workers Party. The precocious seventeen-year-old energetically attempted to convert London to a purer type of socialism. Their discussions* were endless, and she often referred to their friendship as a "battle." In 1900, on the spur of the moment, Jack married Bessie Maddern, and in 1901, their first daughter was born. Still in contact with Anna, Jack met and fell in love with Charmian Kittredge, and abandoned his wife and children. Initially, Bessie believed that Anna had robbed her of Jack's affections. But it was to Charmian whom Bessie had confided her deepest concerns about her marriage to Jack. This letter to Anna, the woman with whom Jack was, perhaps, most honest, was written in 1901.

"Were ever two souls, with dumb lips, more incongruously matched! ... God must laugh at the mummery."

Dear Anna,

Did I say that the human might be filed in categories? Well, and if I did, let me qualify—not all humans. You elude me. I cannot place you, cannot grasp you. I may boast that of nine out of ten, under given circumstances, I can forecast their action; that of nine out of ten, by their word or action, I may feel the pulse of their hearts. But of the tenth I despair. It is beyond me. You are that tenth.

Were ever two souls, with dumb lips, more incongruously matched! We may feel in common—surely, we oftimes do—and when we do not feel in common, yet do we understand; and yet we have no common tongue. Spoken words do not come to us. We are unintelligible. God must laugh at the mummery.

The one gleam of sanity through it all is that we are both large temperamentally, large enough to often understand. True, we often understand but in vague glimmering ways, by dim perceptions, like ghosts, which, while we doubt, haunt us with their truth. And still, I, for one, dare not believe; for you are that tenth which I may not forecast.

Am I unintelligible now? I do not know. I imagine so. I cannot find the common tongue.

Large temperamentally—that is it. It is the one thing that brings us at all in touch. We have, flashed through us, you and I, each a bit of universal, and so we draw together. And yet we are so different.

I smile at you when you grow enthusiastic? It is a forgivable smile—nay, almost an envious smile. I have lived twenty-five years of repression. I learned not to be enthusiastic. It is a hard lesson to forget. I begin to forget, but it is so little. At the best, before I die, I cannot hope to forget all or most. I can exult, now that I am learning, in little things, in other things; but of my things, and secret things doubly mine, I cannot, I cannot. Do I make myself intelligible? Do you hear my voice? I fear not. There are poseurs. I am the most successful of them all.

Ernest Hemingway to Mary Welsh

"Much love dearest Mary and know I'm not impatient. I'm just desperate."

Ernest Hemingway (1899–1961). Celebrated American author of A Farewell to Arms *(1929),* For Whom the Bell Tolls *(1940), and other twentieth-century masterpieces, awarded the Nobel Prize for literature in 1954. Hemingway wrote the following letter to his future wife, Mary Welsh (1908–1986), from Cuba on April 16, 1945.*

Dearest Pickle: This is just a note so that you'll have some mail anyway tonight. I counted on some sure this morning but none came. Maybe will get some tonight. Guess it is too early for the boat letters so must just be patient. Anyhow have now gotten through the 12th, 13th, 14th, 15th and there are only twelve more days to go. Today I'll get through the 16th . . . Sat.

"It's tough as hell without you and I'm doing it straight but I miss you so [I] could die."

night dined . . . out till about 2 A.M. at a cafe on the water front, drinking practically nothing, and talking about you . . . Woke in the morning feeling wonderful and decided would shoot to see how the reflexes were comeing on. Shot fast and very secure. Won 38 bucks. Beat twenty other shooters and was beaten finally in the shoot-off by a bird I killed dead and shot second barrel in so fast after the first one that knocked bird over the fence. Shooting is of no importance and I don't give it any importance and don't want to bore you with accts. of same. But it is a hell of a good sign in the way your property is comeing along. There was a big breeze and the birds fast . . . Am going into town for lunch and Lord it a little tiny bit over the other shooters (with becomeing modesty). It was such good fun to make a comeback . . . I know absolutely the writing will work out the same way. Three weeks ago anybody seeing me shoot pigeons would give you odds I'd never, never come back. And yesterday was faster than steel trap. Pickle you'll just have to have confidence in the writing thing. I know you will have.

You know I realize now I've saved 90 percent of this town and all the fun there is to do and have in it all my life for you. I think you will be crazy about it. If only we were liveing these days instead of just killing them waiting for you to get down here. [The next day, Hemingway continues:] Stayed in last night instead of going out to dinner because thought there might be mail. But there wasn't. And then was sure sure there would be some this morning. There had to be. Today was the 17th and you got in on the 12th. But guess what? There wasn't any mail.

So now I'm going out on the boat with Paxthe and Don Andres and Gregorio and stay out all day and then come in and will be sure there will be letters or a letter. And maybe there will be. If there aren't I'll be a sad s.o.a.b. But you know how you handle that of course? You last through until the next morning. I suppose I'd better figure on there being nothing until tomorrow night and then it won't be so bad tonight . . . Please write me Pickle. If it were a job you had to do you'd do it. It's tough as hell without you and I'm doing it straight but I miss you so [I] could die. If anything happened to you I'd die the way an animal will die in the Zoo if something happens to his mate. [Concluding in holograph:] Will send this with Juan. Much love dearest Mary and know I'm not impatient. I'm just desperate.

Hemingway first met the vivacious and intelligent Mary Welsh in May 1944 while she was a London correspondent for Time *magazine. At that time, his marriage to Martha Gellhorn was already on the skids and ended when she displayed an insensitive bedside manner while visiting Hemingway in a London hospital after a serious automobile accident. He became infatuated with Mary and was reunited with her after the liberation of Paris. She knew her man well, once remarking, "I* wanted him to be the master, to be stronger and cleverer than I, to remember constantly how big he was and how small I was." In fact, they often signed their letters as "Big Kittner" and "Little Kittner."

Though friends expected their marriage in 1946 to collapse quickly, it endured until July 1961 when Hemingway committed suicide.

Zelda Fitzgerald to
F. Scott Fitzgerald

"I could never do without you . . ."

Zelda Fitzgerald (nee Sayre; 1900–1948). American novelist. The beautiful daughter of a well-to-do family from Montgomery, Alabama, Zelda was a free-spirited, rebellious girl when she met author F. Scott Fitzgerald (1896–1940) in July 1918. He noted in his journal that on September 7th he fell in love with Zelda, and the two were married in a small ceremony at New York's St. Patrick's Cathedral in April 1920. A failed ballet dancer and artist, she had a modestly successful career as a novelist, her most famous work being Save Me the Waltz *(1932), which she wrote at Phipps Clinic in Baltimore, while recovering from her second mental breakdown. From the very beginning, the two carried on an extremely codependent, unhealthy, yet enduring and intense love affair. Diagnosed as a schizophrenic, she died in a fire at the Highland Hospital sanitarium where she had been admitted for depression. Fitzgerald once wrote to*

F. Scott and Zelda Fitzgerald

one of Zelda's doctors, "Perhaps fifty percent of our friends and relatives would tell you in all honest conviction that my drinking drove Zelda insane—the other half would assure you that her insanity drove me to drink. Neither judgement would mean anything."

"Without you, dearest dearest I couldn't see or hear or feel or think—or live—I love you so and I'm never in all our lives going to let us be apart another night."

I look down the tracks and see you coming—and out of every haze & mist your darling rumpled trousers are hurrying to me—Without you, dearest dearest I couldn't see or hear or feel or think—or live—I love you so and I'm never in all our lives going to let us be apart another night. It's like begging for mercy of a storm or killing Beauty or growing old, without you. I want to kiss you so—and in the back where your dear hair starts and your chest—I love you—and I can't tell you how much—To think that I'll *die* without your knowing—Goofo, you've *got* to try [to] feel how much I do—how inanimate I am when you're gone—I can't even hate these damnable people—Nobody's got any right to live but us—and they're dirtying up our world and I can't hate them because I want you so—Come Quick—Come Quick to me—I could never do without you if you hated me and were covered with sores like a leper—if you ran away with another woman and starved me and beat me—I still would want you I *know*—Lover, Lover, Darling—Your Wife

Marc Chagall to
Bella Chagall

"... when I sleep all covered with colors, in a bed of pictures ..."

Marc Chagall (1887–1985). Russian-born, French artist known for his highly personal, fantastical images based on Russian-Jewish folk themes and village life. The poem "To Bella" was written in French about two subjects very close to the painter's heart—his art and his devotion to his wife, Bella (nee Rosenfeld), of thirty years. The two first met in October 1909. Bella was the sophisticated and intelligent daughter of a prosperous Jewish family from Vitebsk, Russia, and after marrying Chagall, she became both his inspiration and salvation. She was the fuel of the inner passion that, when ignited, revealed itself in his glorious paintings. He once noted, "I had only to open the window of my room and blue air, love, and flowers entered with her. All dressed in white or else in black, she has flown for a long time over my canvases, guiding my art. I never complete a painting or an engraving without asking for her 'yes' or 'no.'"

To Bella

However my sun shines at night
when I sleep all covered with colors,
in a bed of pictures,
when your foot in my mouth
chokes me, tortures me.

I awake in despair
of a new day, of my still undeveloped,
colorless desires.
I run up there,
towards my dry brushes
and, like Christ, I am crucified,
nailed to my easel.

Am I dead, I myself?
Is my picture finished?
Everything shines, everything clings, everything flows.
Stop! Another dab
of black.
Red, blue have settled in
and this worries me.

Listen to me
funeral bed,
parched grass,
dying love.
To a new beginning
Listen to me.

Vita Sackville-West to Virginia Woolf

"I am reduced to a thing that wants Virginia."

Vita Sackville-West (1892–1962). English poet and novelist, author of The Edwardians *(1930) and* All Passion Spent *(1931). She married diplomat and author Harold Nicolson in 1913, and their passionless union endured despite numerous homosexual affairs, including Vita's longstanding relationship with her childhood friend, Violet Trefusis, the daughter of Alice Keppel, King Edward the VII's mistress. First introduced to fellow novelist Virginia Woolf through Virginia's brother-in-law, Clive Bell, their intimate friendship was one of the central relationships of London's Bloomsbury Group, a pre–World War I literary and artistic community. Vita was the inspiration for Virginia's masterpiece,* Orlando *(1928). After Sackville-West's death, her son Nigel published* Portrait of a Marriage, *based on his mother's journal detailing the loving friendship she had with her husband along with her affairs with other women. The following letter to Virginia was sent from Milan on January 21, 1927.*

"It is incredible how essential to me you have become."

. . . I am reduced to a thing that wants Virginia. I composed a beautiful letter to you in the sleepless nightmare hours of the night, and it has all gone: I just miss you, in a quite simple desperate human way. You, with all your undumb letters, would never write so elementary a phrase as that; perhaps you wouldn't even feel it. And yet I believe you'll be sensible of a little gap. But you'd clothe it in so exquisite a phrase that it would lose a little of its reality. Whereas with me it is quite stark: I miss you even more than I could have believed; and I was prepared to miss you a good deal. So this letter is really just a squeal of pain. It is incredible how essential to me you have become. I suppose you are accustomed to people saying these things. Damn you, spoilt creature; I shan't make you love me any the more by giving myself away like this—But oh my dear, I can't be clever and stand-offish with you: I love you too much for that. Too truly. You have no idea how stand-offish I can be with people I don't love. I have brought it to a fine art. But you have broken down my defences. And I don't really resent it.

Virginia Woolf

Virginia Woolf (1882–1941). British novelist, essayist, critic, feminist, socialist, pacifist, and one of the leaders in the modernist movement. Author of To the Lighthouse *(1927),* Mrs. Dalloway *(1925), and* Jacob's Room *(1922), Virginia was an equally ardent admirer of Vita, describing her in her journal as a "grenadier; hard; handsome; manly . . ." who made her feel "virgin shy & schoolgirlish . . ." The following letter was written to Vita in 1927.*

Look Here Vita—throw over your man, and we'll go to Hampton Court and dine on the river together and walk in the garden in the moonlight and come home late and have a bottle of wine and get tipsy, and I'll tell you all the things I have in my head, millions, myriads—They won't stir by day, only by dark on the river. Think of that. Throw over your man, I say, and come.

Alfred de Musset to George Sand

"I have something stupid and ridiculous to tell you."

Alfred de Musset (1810–1857). French Romantic poet and playwright, whose work, unlike that of many of his contemporaries, is still widely read and performed. His brief and turbulent affair with the novelist George Sand (pseudonym of Amandine Aurore Lucile Dupin, baronne Dudevant; 1804–1876), the recipient of this 1833 letter, inspired many of his finest poems.

My dear George,

I have something stupid and ridiculous to tell you. I am foolishly writing you instead of telling you this, I do not know why, when returning from that walk. Tonight I shall be annoyed at having done so. You will laugh in my face, will take me for a phrase-maker in all my relations with you hitherto. You will show me the door and you will think I am lying. I am in love with you.

This letter from the twenty-three-year-old Parisian dandy to the already celebrated author George Sand, who was six years his senior, marks the beginning of a brief and unusual affair. Leaving her two children behind, Sand and Musset departed for Venice after a brief fling at Fontainebleau. On January 19, 1834, they checked into Venice's Hotel Danieli, but by then they were already quarreling. They quickly realized that their infatuation was not love, and to complicate matters Musset fell seriously ill with typhoid. With the aid of a young, handsome, though not terribly bright Italian doctor named Pagello, Sand was left to nurse him back to health (as she later would do with Chopin). Sand and Musset still argued vehemently, and they finally parted company, with Musset returning to France. By then, Sand had found a new lover—Doctor Pagello—and she lingered a bit longer in Italy.

Poster for Musset's play *Lorenzaccio*

Jack Kerouac to
Sebastian Sampas

"You magnificent bastard!"

Jean Louis "Jack" Kerouac (1922–1969). American poet and novelist of French-Canadian descent. Jack briefly studied at Columbia University, served in the U.S. Navy until discharged for emotional reasons, and then joined the Merchant Marine. He held a variety of jobs as he traveled throughout the United States and Mexico. He considered his first novel, The Town and the City *(1950), too conventional, and he began to experiment with a more liberated and spontaneous style in his next work,* On the Road *(1957), a semi-autobiographical tale, written in just three weeks, detailing his wanderings across the United States with Neal Cassady. The novel instantly established Jack's reputation as a spokesman for the Beat Generation, but he was unable to cope with the enormous attention he received as a result of the book's popularity. His political views became increasingly conservative (he supported the*

Vietnam War) and his personal life more self-destructive. Jack married his third wife, Stella Sampas, in 1966 and spent his final years with his mother and wife, in Lowell, Massachusetts, and later in St. Petersburg, Florida, where he died in 1969. Stella was the sister of Sebastian Sampas, Kerouac's childhood friend, and a fellow poet. He is the recipient of the following letter written in March 1943.

Sebastian!

You magnificent bastard! I was just thinking about you, and all of a sudden, I feel

very Sebastianish,
very Bohemian!
very Baroque!
very GAY!   (TURN!)

I was thinking, in a flash of glory, about all the things we've done!!!—and all the others we're going to do!

AFTER THE WAR, WE MUST GO TO FRANCE AND SEE THAT THE REVOLUTION GOES WELL!   AND GERMANY TOO! AND ITALY TOO! AND *RUSSIA*!

For 1. Vodka
    2. Love
    3. Glory.

We must find Pat Reel and get drunk with him; we must get tanked up with Phillipe: like Paxton Hibben, we must lay a wreath on Jack Reed's grave in Moscow—

Harvard boy—died in MOSCOW!

Sebastian you son of a beetch!

HOW ARE YOU?

I AM DRUNK!

Do you hear me? Do not die, *live*! We must go to Paris and see that the revolution goes well! And the counter-revolutions in GERMANY, SPAIN, ITALY, YUGOSLAVIA, POLAND ETC.ETC.ETC.

We must go to Bataan and pick a flower. . . .

SEBASTIAN!

SYMPATHY!

To hell with
>   La Bourgeoisie!

No, *La Bourgueosie!*

To hell with
>   Hearst

To hell with
>   Everything

That does not
>   add up
>   TO

Brothers living together and laughing their labours to fruition!

DECK THYSELF *NOW* WITH MAJESTY AND EXCEL-LENCY: CAST DOWN THE WICKED IN THEIR PLACE . . .

Au diable
>   *AVEC*

les cochons capitalistes,

y los cabrones
>   *científicos!*

STRUMBOUTSOMOUGAVALA
>   *with the Salops Riches!*

SYMPATHIE!
C'est le bon mot . . .
C'est le seul mot . . .
La Sympathie et l'humeur—
J'AIME MES FRÈRES:
ILS SONT TRAGIQUES,
BEAUX, BONS, Beaucoup de noblesse—
A l'avant!
Sebastian:—

Red Wine, I have just written to Norma, my Gretchen, my Humanist—Socialist—Psychologist—Amorous love!

This isn't folly, this is me! I am mad with ardor for all things AND Sebastian!

THE LEAF UNTURNED

In a month or so, if I don't hear from the Navy, I shall ship out, I shall go to Camp Lee, and see you, I shall infuse you with new hope. You're not cheated! You're magnificent!

JEAN Louis le Brise de Kerouac, Baron de Bretagne, retired. AU REVOIR.

John Rodgers to Minerva Denison

"the magnetic power of your charms . . ."

*John Rodgers (1773–1838). The highest-ranking American naval offi-
cer during the War of 1812 and U.S. Secretary of the Navy in 1823.
This rapturous letter from December 17, 1802, in which John declares
his love for his future wife, Minerva Denison, was written while serving
in the Mediterranean during the Tripolitan War, where he distinguished
himself as the commander of the blockade that brought about peace.
Though the conflict afforded him only one brief visit to the United States
between 1802 and 1806, John's missives won Minerva's heart, and the
two were married upon his return to America.*

There is no command you could have charg'd me with so
severe as to deny me the priviledge of a correspondence,
except you were with contempt to command me to relinquish

that sensibility, of which <u>Heaven</u> was the founder and a <u>Divinity</u> the chief Architect. From retrospective recollection I can still figure to my imagination every branch and leaf of the unfeeling little peach tree, in presence of, and under which, your sensible heart, altho cruel tongue pass'd the agonizing sentence of denying me the priviledge of a communication by letter. But Minerva, did you possess the power of the wise idol whose name you bear? My love for you is such as would (in this instance) force me to disobey you, without giving me greater proofs, that your contempt for me is as arbitrary as your commands were cruel and decisive. I am not afraid to face the enemies of my country, even, in the shape of furies from Hell, and could you suspect me of being coward enough to submit with pusillanimity to a charge so directly in disunion with my soul. 'Tis often said by the good people of Terra Firma that salt water and long absence cures all pains to which sailors' hearts are subject. With the candor of one of Neptune's pupils, I honestly confess it had always been the case with me, until I had the happiness or unhappiness to be honor'd with your acquaintance. However, I will not despair nor be so profane as to accuse the all wise supreme of injustice until you give me more sufficient reason. I am now on a part of the globe where even the compass itself is false, as all points have revoked their constancy, since I left America, and chang'd their direction upwards of twenty degrees to embrace some nearer object. But Minerva (forgive the familiar appellation) the magnetic power of your charms have to this moment prevented my heart from varying a single second. I know no art in love as you may plainly discover by the diction of my scribbling, but the professions I have made were dictated by a heart as honest, as

"But Minerva (forgive the familiar appellation) the magnetic power of your charms have to this moment prevented my heart from varying a single second."

proud, and as honorable as that of any other being in existence, and if to possess such feelings be a crime, the errors are not mine but his who made us both. I feel my intellect so perfectly inadequate to an expression of the sensations I feel, that I am oblig'd with painful reluctance to drop the subject. Further than to ask you to answer me with that perfectly undisguised

Minerva Denison and John Rodgers

and generous candor with which I address you, if you will ever condescend to make me that happy, happy being whom you alone have the power to possess. If your heart has not yet rightly informed you, do not be too precipitate. And beware of making miserable a man that would sacrifice his very existence to make you happy. If you answer me in the negitive <u>Farewell</u> and farewell to the banks of that river where I drew my first breath. We are now bound to Malta, the island where St. Paul was ship wreck'd, and will, in the course of a few days, be in sight of the island of Candia which affords the disasterous subject of the ship wreck. Poor Palemon how I pity him. My <u>Champion</u>, and your old acquaintance, Mr. Smith, is much elated with the romantic scenes of huge mountains, antient Moorish castles, Spanish convents and stupendous rocks which dourly present themselves to his view. We saw the castle of Andalusia a few days ago and Mr. Ratcliff has ever since

U. S. Frigate Siren

Ever estimable Minerva   Almeria Bay, Spain, Decemr 17th 1802

There is no Command you could have
charged me with so severe as to deny me the priviledge of a
correspondence, except you were with Contempt to Command me to
relinquish that Sensibility, of which *Heaven* was the Founder
and A *Divinity* the chief Architect. — From retrospective recollection I can still figure to my Immagination
every branch and leaf of the unfeeling little Peach Tree, in
presence of, and under which, your sensible Heart, altho Cruel
Tongue passd the agonizing sentence Denying me the priviledge of a Communication by letter: but Minerva, did you
possess the power of the wise Idol whose name you bear
— my love for you is such as would in this Instance force
me to disobey you, without giving me greater Proofs, that
your Contempt for me is as arbitrary as your Commands were
cruel and Decisive: I am not afraid to face the Enemies
of my Country, even in the shape of Furies from Hell, and
could You suspect me of being Coward Enough to submit
with Pusillanimity to a Charge so Directly in Disunion
with My Soul. — 'Tis often said by the good People of
Terra Firma, that salt water and long absence Cures al

Pains

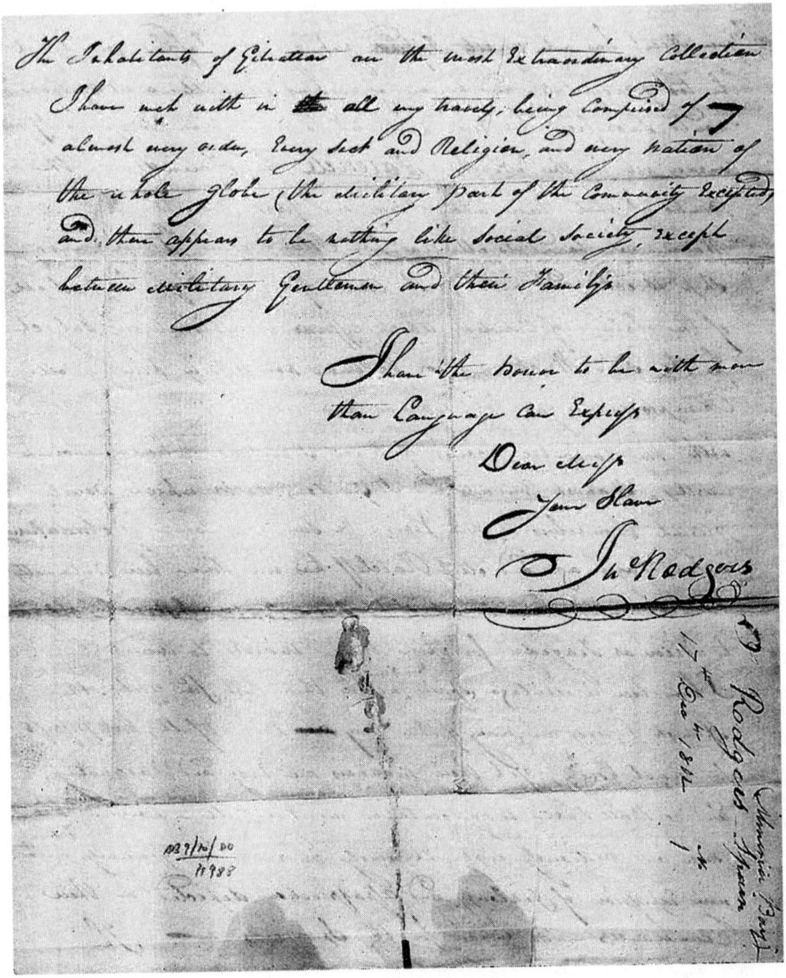

been continually in his mouth. However what he sees as comedy I shall be obliged to view as tragedy for these nine months to come. I have been in Malaga, Spain, via Gibraltar, within these last five weeks. The Spanish ladies are, many of them, very beautiful, but possess too much levity, yet their manners are lazy and fascinating, and as ballroom acquaintances are very well. However, the men are hideously ugly, extremely uncouth, and generally with every expression of jealousy and assassination depicted in their countenances. So much for Spaniards. The inhabitants of Gibraltar are the most extraordinary collection I have met with in all my travels, being comprised of almost every order, every sect and religion, and every nation of the whole globe (the military part of the community excepted) and there appears to be nothing like social society, except between military gentlemen and their family's. I have the honor to be with more than language can express, dear miss, your slave . . .

A well-suited pair, John and Minerva were both descended from distinguished, seafaring families. After marrying, John gained popularity for defeating the British aboard the U.S.S. President *in 1811, and his effective performance throughout the War of 1812 earned him a presidential appointment as head of the Board of Naval Commissioners—a post he held for many years. John's son and namesake followed in his father's footsteps by serving in the navy during the Seminole wars and Civil War, attaining the rank of rear admiral.*

Alfred Dreyfus to Lucie Dreyfus

"Even to-day I feel that I must be the victim of some frightful nightmare . . ."

Alfred Dreyfus (1859–1935). A French-Jewish army officer born in Mulhouse, France, best remembered for his arrest for treason, which initiated a twelve-year controversy widely known as the Dreyfus Affair. An artillery captain on the General Staff, Alfred was falsely accused of selling French military secrets to the Germans in 1894. While in prison, and just prior to his banishment to Devil's Island, he wrote his wife Lucie (nee Hadomard) about his love for her, his suffering, and his desire to obtain justice. The ongoing efforts of his wife, brother, and friends to prove his innocence only continued to provoke a vigorous anti-Semitic response, and deeply divide the French intellectual and political world. The case was retried in 1899, where Alfred was found guilty again (of "treason under extenuating circumstances"). In a judicial surprise,

Dreyfus was offered a pardon, which he reluctantly accepted. Finally, in 1906, the verdict was overturned, and all charges were dropped, including those against officers in the French military who had conspired to implicate and convict Alfred. Incontrovertible proof came in 1930 when declassified German military documents revealed his innocence.

Tuesday December 5, 1894

My Dear Lucie,

At last I can send you word. I have just been told that my trial is set for the 19th of this month. I am denied the right to see you. I will not tell you all that I have suffered; there are not in the world words strong enough to give expression to it. Do you remember when I used to tell you how happy we were? Everything in life smiled on us. Then of a sudden came a thunderbolt which left my brain reeling. To be accused of the most monstrous crime that a soldier can commit! Even to-day I feel that I must be the victim of some frightful nightmare. . . .

But I trust in God's justice. In the end truth must prevail. My conscience does not reproach me. I have always done my duty; never have I turned from it. Crushed down in this sombre cell, alone with my reeling brain, I have had moments when I have been beside myself; but even then my conscience was on guard. "Hold up thy head!" it said to me. "Look the world in the face! Strong in thy consciousness of right, rise up, go straight on! This trial is frightfully bitter, but it must be endured!"

I embrace you a thousand times, as I love you, as I adore you, my darling Lucie.

A thousand kisses to the children. I dare not say more about them to you; the tears come into my eyes when I think of them.
Alfred

"I am denied the right to see you. I will not tell you all that I have suffered... I adore you, my darling Lucie."

Marjorie Fossa
to Elvis Presley

"I AM NOW ON CLOUD 9,000."

Marjorie Fossa (dates unavailable). Contrary to what many might think, fan letters are not a new phenomenon. The deeply gratifying and lasting relationships of both Balzac and Browning, for example, had their origins in fan letters, so it seemed appropriate to include one in this anthology. This letter was written to one of America's most enduring legends, Elvis Presley (1935–1977), on June 12, 1972, the year of "Burning Love," his last Top 10 hit. Although Marjorie may be expressing herself in a less poetic way than Robert Browning ever did to Elizabeth Barrett, there is a compelling honesty in her prose. What must "The King" have thought when he read the line, "I love you for what you are . . . not for who you are"? Marjorie says the King responded with a thank-you note and an autographed photo, both of which she keeps carefully locked away in her safe deposit box.

Dear Elvis,

ALAS, AT LONG LAST I FINALLY SAW YOU IN CONCERT SAT. JUNE 10th AT MADISON SQUARE GARDEN.

I AM NOW ON CLOUD 9,000.

I cannot eat, sleep, drive or function at all. I have been a devout fan and admirer of you since the first day you hit the scene in the fifties. I have never liked music by anyone else. I have lost lots of boyfriends through high school (only because they were all jealous of you). I have spent all of my allowance on your records. I worked three part-time jobs in school just so that I could continue buying all of your music and anything else that I could get my hands on. I was in high school through the fifties, was later married in 1960 (to a soldier no less) and believe it or not he does look a lot like you, but not nearly as handsome. I have traveled all over in hopes of seeing you some-day (I never gave up). I lived in Washington, DC, Virginia, Oklahoma, and now in NJ. When I heard you were appearing at the Garden, I immediately arranged to take a day off work in order to go to the city and get as many tickets as I could. You see, all of my friends are also fans of yours. (I wouldn't think of having any other friends of course). Needless to say our tickets for seats were all the way up to the sky, but I purchased a pair of high-powered binoculars so that I could see you as close as possible. Girls were being dragged and/or carried out by the NYC PD, the day was the most exciting day of my life (more so than my wedding day).

Incidentally, my husband accompanied me to your concert and he did not care that much for you UNTIL HE SAW YOU AT THE GARDEN and now he is a great fan also and even

"I worked three part-time jobs in school just so that I could continue buying all of your music and any-thing else that I could get my hands on."

admitted to me that I have great taste. Before he would not allow me to play your records while he was home. I always had to wait for him to leave so I could play your music. This did not make me happy and I threatened to divorce him if he didn't straighten out and let me have a life too.

I returned to my job today . . . A big surprise was waiting for me. I had worked for this crummy building contractor for one year and he did not mind my taking a day off, but the idea that I had gone to get tickets to see you. I am so furious that I hope he can't find another secretary to replace me. But in the end result IT WAS WORTH LOSING FIFTY JOBS. I love you more than life itself and I can't wait to see you in concert again. Keep coming to NYC. When my husband sat there and watched the Garden fill up to capacity, he decided that you had to be great for so many followers to be there admiring you and screaming and yelling.

I LOVE YOU FOR WHAT YOU ARE AND THE WAY YOU PLEASE THOUSANDS OF PEOPLE THE WORLD OVER, NOT FOR WHO YOU ARE. When I was young I used to dream of being Mrs. Presley, like all other teenage girls I suppose. YOU have made the greatest impact on people and the music business, not only rock 'n' roll, I enjoy every song that you sing. You have a magnetism like no other. I will close for now. I hope you never stop singing, you truly make this world a better place, there should be more in it like you, but there could never be another to replace you, I'll spend my whole life through "LOVING YOU."

Your #1 Fan
Marjorie Fossa
Montclair, New Jersey

Passionate Prose

Honoré de Balzac to Éveline Hanska

"My beloved Angel"

Honoré de Balzac (1799–1850). French-born novelist. A highly original writer whose extensive creative output reflected many aspects of French society, Balzac is best known for his monumental The Human Comedy, *which he began in 1834 and which occupied him for most of his remaining years. Balzac's love life was no less fascinating than the scandalous villains of his stories and novels. At the tender age of twenty-three, he embarked on a liaison with a woman nearly twice his age, Mme. Berny, known as "la Dilecta." Her influence on Balzac (the noble appellation "de" was an affectation that Balzac personally awarded himself) was no doubt beneficial. But in 1832, he entered into a less satisfying relationship with the Marquise de Castries, a woman he unflatteringly portrayed in the* Duchesse de Langeais. *That same year, he received a fan letter from a married Polish noble woman, Countess Éveline Hanska. A*

Honoré de Balzac

correspondence ensued, and they met twice in Switzerland in 1833, and in Vienna two years later. He came to refer to her as "The Foreigner," and the two promised to marry each other once her husband died. Their relationship endured for seventeen years, and their correspondence, collected in the four-volume Letters to a Foreigner, *is one of the great examples of epistolary love. Although the Count died in 1842, the couple was thwarted by Balzac's precarious finances. Finally, in March 1850, when he was already mortally ill, the two wed. Balzac died in Paris five months later.*

June 1835

MY BELOVED ANGEL,

I am nearly mad about you, as much as one can be mad: I cannot bring together two ideas that you do not interpose yourself between them. I can no longer think of nothing but you. In spite of myself, my imagination carries me to you. I grasp you, I kiss you, I caress you, a thousand of the most amorous caresses take possession of me. As for my heart, there you will always be—very much so. I have a delicious sense of you there. But my God, what is to become of me, if you have deprived me of my reason. This is a monomania which, this morning, terrifies me. I rise up every moment saying to myself, "Come, I am going there!" Then I sit down again, moved by the sense of my obligations. There is a frightful conflict. This is not life. I have never before been like that. You have devoured everything. I feel foolish and happy as soon as I let myself think of you. I whirl round in a delicious dream in which in one instant I live a thousand years. What a horrible situation! Overcome with love, feeling love in every pore, living only for love, and seeing oneself consumed by griefs, and caught in a thousand spiders' threads. O, my darling Eva, you did not know it. I picked up your card. It is there before me, and I talked to you as if you were there. I see you, as I did yesterday, beautiful, astonishingly beautiful. Yesterday, during the whole evening, I said to myself "She is mine!" Ah! The angels are not as happy in Paradise as I was yesterday!

Ludwig van Beethoven to the "Immortal Beloved"

"My angel, my all"

Ludwig van Beethoven (1770–1827). German composer and the predominant musical figure in the transitional period between the Classical and Romantic eras. A student of both Wolfgang Amadeus Mozart and Joseph Haydn, Beethoven is considered one of the titanic figures in the history of music. Never married, he nevertheless fell in love several times—usually with women who were married, unobtainable, or otherwise inappropriate. In 1811, in poor health, Beethoven traveled to the spa in Teplitz, returning to Vienna refreshed and ready to commence work on his 7th Symphony, which he finished in the spring of 1812. On July 5, 1812, he returned to Teplitz and, over the course of the next two days, composed one of the most remarkable love letters ever written. The letter was addressed to the unnamed "unsterbliche Geliebte," or "immortal Beloved." This exceptional letter was found among Beethoven's personal effects after his death. It had never been *sent. The only known love letter by Beethoven using the familiar "du" for "you," and first published in 1840, the identity of its mysterious recipient has been the subject of entire books. Over the years, many of Beethoven's biographers have arrived at possible solutions for solving the puzzle. Current research points to Antonie Brentano, an aristocratic Viennese lady he had known since 1810, who was married to a Frankfurt businessman.*

My angel, my all, my very self.—Only a few words today, and, what is more, written in pencil (and with your pencil)—I shan't be certain of my rooms here until tomorrow; what an unnecessary waste of time is all this—Why this profound sorrow, when necessity speaks—can our love endure without

"My heart overflows with a longing to tell you so many things— Oh—there are moments when I find that speech is quite inadequate—"

sacrifices, without our demanding everything from one another; can you alter the fact that you are not wholly mine, that I am not wholly yours?—Dear God, look at Nature in all her beauty and set your heart at rest about what must be—Love demands all, and rightly so, and thus it is for me with you, for you with me—But you forget so easily that I must live for me and for you; if we were completely united, you would feel this painful necessity just as little as I do. No doubt we shall meet soon; and today also time fails me to tell you of the thoughts which during these last few days I have been revolving about my life—If our hearts were always closely united, I would certainly entertain no such thoughts. My heart overflows with a longing to tell you so many things—Oh—there are moments when I find that speech is quite inadequate—Be cheerful—and be for ever my faithful, my only sweetheart, my all, as I am yours. The gods must send us everything else, whatever must and shall be our fate—your faithful Ludwig

Monday evening, July 6th

You are suffering, you, my most precious one—I have noticed this very moment that letters have to be handed in very early, on Monday—or on Thursday—the only days when the mail coach goes from here to K.—You are suffering—Oh, where I am, you are with me—I will see to it that you and I, that I can live with you. What a life!!!! as it is now!!!! without you—pursued by the kindness of people here and there, a kindness that I think—that I wish to deserve just as little as I deserve it—man's homage to man—that pains me—and when I consider myself in the setting of the universe, what am I and what is that man—whom one calls the greatest of men—and yet—on the other hand therein lies the divine element in man— I weep when I think that probably you will not receive the first news of me until Saturday—However much you love me—my

"Your love has made me both the happiest and unhappiest of mortals—At my age I now need stability and regularity in my life— can this coexist with our relationship?"

love for you is even greater —but never conceal yourself from me—good night.—Dear God—so near! so far! Is not our love truly founded in Heaven—and, what is more, as strongly cemented as the firmament of heaven?—

Good morning, on July 7th

Even when I am in bed my thoughts rush to you, my immortal beloved, now and then joyfully, then again sadly, waiting to know whether Fate will hear our prayer—To face life I must live altogether with you or never see you. Yes, I am resolved to be a wanderer abroad until I can fly to your arms and say that I have found my true home with you and enfolded in your arms let my soul be wafted to the realm of blessed spirits—alas, unfortunately it must be so—You will become composed, the more so as you know that I am faithful to you; no other woman can ever possess my heart—never—never—Oh God, why must one be separated from her who is so dear. Yet my life in V[ienna] at present is a miserable life—Your love has made me both the happiest and unhappiest of mortals—At my age I now need stability and regularity in my life—can this coexist with our relationship?—Angel, I have just heard that the post goes every day—and therefore I must close, so that you may receive the letter immediately—Be calm; for only by calmly considering our lives can we achieve our purpose to live together—be calm—love me—Today—yesterday—what tearful longing for you—for you—you—my life—my all—all good wishes to you—Oh, do continue to love me—never misjudge your lover's most faithful heart.

ever yours

ever mine

ever ours

Robert Browning to George Barrett

"She laughed with pleasure . . ."

Robert Browning (1812–1889). English Victorian poet. Born to a well-read father and a mother who was an accomplished pianist, the young Browning was an extremely bright child who, by the age of fourteen, had written a volume of Byronic verse, and knew Latin, Greek, French, and Italian. In 1846, against the wishes of her domineering father, he secretly married the poet Elizabeth Barrett, and left for Italy where they spent the next fifteen years living happily but in virtual seclusion. A master of the dramatic monologue, his finest book of poetry, Men and Women *(1855), was dedicated to his wife. An invalid since her youth, Elizabeth died in her husband's arms on June 30, 1861. This moving account of her final days was written from Florence two days later, and sent to her brother George. Robert returned to London with their son, where his masterpiece,* The Ring and the Book, *appeared in 1869. He died on*

the day that his final volume of poetry, Asolando, *was published.*
Robert is buried in Westminster Abbey's poets' corner.

You must not hate me for giving you any pain anybody else
might have spared you,—tho' I am too stupid to tell how. She
was never "ill," arrived "well," had the news of Cavour's death
next day and was prostrated by it—recovering, I suppose, only
partially when she caught cold "the usual attack, no worse," was
never in bed in the day time, till the last day, and then by a com-
bination of circumstances which kept her from going into the
drawing room and kept assuring us that the doctor was wrong
with his serious view of the case until the end came. The last
evening Wilson (the maid) came to see her & went away satisfied nothing would happen. My instinct knew better, all the
while, but my reason was justified in believing her assurances
that she would "certainly soon be well again." The last evening
she wanted me to take and furnish a Villa for three years. Thro'
the night she repeated she was better, "comfortable," "beautiful"—bidding me "only come to bed now—why stay up now?" I
knew the worst was impending by some instinct, I repeat—for I
could explain away every ill symptom,—a little wandering, after
a weeks absolute refusal of solid food, and a (prescribed) slight
addition to the morphine dose, what was in that? The frightful
thing, really, was only the vehement expression of her perfect
love for me when, if nothing was to happen, there would be
nothing to account for it in my simply standing beside her—but
I will say, in profound gratitude, that her last words were bidding "God bless me" in tones and with what never accompanied
any words of hers to me before. She laughed with pleasure and
youth, and I believe in some perfectly gracious way allowed by

God suffered no pain whatever, even as she averred. Had you been in the next house I don't think I should have called you

"I am absolutely alone..."

in—but I sate up myself every night but one—unknown to her, who supposed I slept on a sofa, to please my inward misgivings, for the most part, rather than satisfy any so apparent need. The best Doctor we have, stayed with us till morning the first night and supposed the difficulty was over and that "sleep now" would mend all: then he found out that one lung was solidified—the right. "The left, Dr. Chambers would have it"—she replied—"it's the old experience I've had in plenty—they don't understand" and I was bound to hope they did not: the worst he remarked was—"If I were not assured this is a very exceptional case, and I did not know that there are such cases, I should suspect an abscess on the lungs. She is however certainly better today, better again this evening—and so on. The last night she sate up by herself, cleaned her teeth, washed her face and combed her hair without the least assistance—and she took two servings of jelly from me spoonful by spoonful and drank a glass of lemonade not a quarter of an hour before the end: this is all I can bear to tell you now of it, and I bear so much only to be relieved of your just reproach if my silence to you had arisen from disregard of an obviously impending calamity. She was buried yesterday—with the shops in the street shut, a crowd of people following sobbing, another crowd of Italians, Americans & English crying like children at the cemetery, for they knew who she was—"the greatest English Poet of the day, writer of the sublimest poem ever penned by a woman, and Italy's truest and dearest of friends"—as the morning and evening papers told them, "calling on the friends of Art & Italy, of whatever tribe and sect, to go and pay a last homage"—& so they did, I am told, for I saw nothing but for one minute a flash of faces—noble, grateful Italians.

I have nothing more to do with Italy for many a year, however. I shall go at once to England, or rather Paris first, and then London: I shall give myself wholly up to the care & education of our child; I know all Ba's mind as to how that should be, and shall try and carry out her desires—I have formed no particular plan as yet, but am certain enough of the main direction my life will take: but there is much to wind up here before I can go away with the relief of knowing that I need not return in a hurry . . .

Wednesday. I must write no more letters like this. I propose to go to England the moment I can wind up my affairs here, and to see Arabel for a few days: I shall then be able to say as much as I ought to say & no more—which I cannot manage now. For the last time, all brothers & relatives must forgive my not attempting to write them—I am absolutely alone—with much help of another kind, and every sort of offered assistance, but I cannot yet go over this again & again in letters . . .

Katherine Mansfield to John Middleton Murry

"... so perfect is my love for you ..."

Katherine Mansfield (1888–1923). A short story writer born in New Zealand. Katherine attended Queen's College in London, returned home briefly to study music, but then went back to London to pursue a literary career. Distraught by the death of her brother Leslie during World War I, she wrote her first major work, Prelude *(1917), in remembrance of their childhood and native country.* Prelude *was a collection of her stories and reviews published at Virginia and Leonard Woolf's Hogarth Press. After an early and unsuccessful marriage to George Bowden, she married, in 1918, writer John Middleton Murry (1889–1957), the recipient of this letter from May 18, 1917. Later, Katherine became involved with a select literary community including D. H. Lawrence and Virginia Woolf. Her finest and most influential work was written during her final years. She died from tuberculosis in 1923 at the age of thirty-five.*

My Darling

Do not imagine, because you find these lines in your private book that I have been trespassing. You know I have not—and where else shall I leave a love letter? For I long to write you a love letter tonight. You are all about me—I seem to breathe

"—and so perfect is my love for you that I am, as it were, still, silent to my very soul."

you—hear you—feel you in me and of me—What am I doing here? You are away—I have seen you in the train, at the station, driving up, sitting in the lamplight talking, greeting people—washing your hands—And I am here—in your tent—sitting at your table. There are some wallflower petals on the table and a dead match, a blue pencil and a *Magdeburgische Zeitung*. I am just as much at home as they.

When dusk came—flowing up the silent garden—lapping against the blind windows—my first & last terror started up—I was making some coffee in the kitchen. It was so violent, so dreadful I put down the coffee-pot—and simply ran away—ran out of the studio and up the street with my bag under one arm and a block of writing paper and a pen under the other. I felt that if I could get here & find Mrs. [illegible] I should be 'safe'—I found her and I lighted your gas, wound up your clock—drew your curtains—& embraced your black overcoat before I sat down—frightened no longer. Do not be angry with me, Bogey—*ca a ete plus forte que moi* . . . That is why I am here.

When you came to tea this afternoon you took a brioche broke it in half & padded the inside doughy bit with two fingers. You always do that with a bun or a roll or a piece of bread—It is your way—your head a little on one side the while . . .

—When you opened your suitcase I saw your old feltie and a French book and a comb all higgledy piggledy—"Tig. I've only got 3 handkerchiefs"—why should that memory be so sweet to me? . . .

Last night, there was a moment before you got into bed. You stood, quite naked, bending forward a little—talking. It was only for an instant. I saw you—I loved you so—loved your body with such tenderness—Ah my dear—And I am not thinking now of 'passion.' No, of that other thing that makes me feel that every inch of you is so precious to me. Your soft shoulders—your creamy warm skin, your ears, cold like shells are cold—your long legs and your feet that I love to clasp with my feet—the feeling of your belly—& your thin young back—Just below that bone that sticks out at the back of your neck you have a little mole. It is partly because we are young that I feel this tenderness—I love your youth—I could not bear that it should be touched even by a cold wind if I were the Lord.

We two, you know have everything before us, and we shall do very great things—I have perfect faith in us—and so perfect is my love for you that I am, as it were, still, silent to my very soul. I want nobody but you for my lover and my friend and to nobody but you shall I be *faithful*.

I am yours for ever.

Tig

Oscar Wilde to

Constance Wilde

"soul and body . . . mingled in some exquisite ecstasy with yours."

Oscar Wilde (1854–1900). Irish poet, wit, and dramatist. Author of The Picture of Dorian Gray _(1891), and_ The Importance of Being Earnest _(1895). This letter from December 1884 is the only known surviving example of Oscar to his wife, Constance (nee Lloyd)._

December 16, 1884

Dear and Beloved, Here am I, and you at the Antipodes. O execrable facts, that keep our lips from kissing, though our souls are one. What can I tell you by letter? Alas! nothing that I would tell you. The message of the gods to each other travel not by pen and ink and indeed your bodily presence here would

Oscar Wilde

"The air is full of the music of your voice, my soul and body seem no longer mine, but mingled in some exquisite ecstasy with yours."

not make you more real: for I feel your fingers in my hair, and your cheek brushing mine. The air is full of the music of your voice, my soul and body seem no longer mine, but mingled in some exquisite ecstasy with yours. I feel incomplete without you. Ever and ever yours, Oscar.

Constance first met Oscar Wilde in 1881, and was immediately charmed. She confided to her brother that when the two were alone, "he's never a bit affected, and speaks naturally," and later announced her engagement proclaiming that she was "insanely happy." Oscar's mother, Lady Wilde, was also pleased for her son. In a letter reminiscent of one of Oscar's slightly overbearing, lightweight, female characters, she wrote that he should have "a small house in London, and live the literary life and teach Constance to correct proofs, and eventually go into

Parliament." The two were married on May 29, 1884, left for Paris on a monthlong honeymoon, and enjoyed several years of happiness, including the birth of two sons, Cyril and Vyvyan. It soon became evident, however, that Constance could neither cope with Oscar's emotional development nor keep up with his brilliance, due to a rather limited intellect and absence of humor. Oscar's homosexuality, and his "ill-fated and most lamentable friendship" with Lord Alfred Douglas that "ended in ruin and public infamy," resulted in a conviction and imprisonment for sodomy that broke his uniquely gentle and sublime spirit.

Frida Kahlo to Diego Rivera

"... all the paths of my nerves which are yours."

Frida Kahlo (1907–1954). Twentieth-century painter. Frida's unique style can be best described as a cross between Mexican folk art and Surrealism. At the age of eighteen, she was involved in a bizarre traffic accident that left her so injured that she endured thirty-five operations throughout the rest of her short life. It was during her painful recovery that she began to teach herself to paint. Photographer Tina Modotti reintroduced Frida to the Mexican artist Diego Rivera (1886–1957), whom she had superficially known since her school days, and the two soon became inseparable. Married in 1929, then briefly separated ten years later, they remarried in 1941. Frida died shortly after her forty-seventh birthday in 1954.

Diego:

Nothing compares to your hands, nothing like the green-gold of your eyes. My body is filled with you for days and days. You are the mirror of the night. the violent flash of lightening. The dampness of the earth. The hollow of your armpits is my shelter. My fingertips touch your blood. All my joy is to feel life spring from your flower-fountain that mine keeps to fill all the paths of my nerves which are yours.

Frida Kahlo and Diego Rivera

Emma Goldman to Ben Reitman

"You have opened up the prison gates of my womanhood."

Emma Goldman (1869–1940). An anarchist, known as "Red Emma." Born in Lithuania, Emma immigrated to the United States in 1885. While working in a Rochester, New York, garment factory, she became aware of unfair labor practices. In 1889, Emma moved to New York City and formed a close relationship with fellow radical, Alexander Berkman, who, in 1892, attempted to assassinate the industrialist Henry Clay Frick and was sent to prison. Emma was one of the most extraordinary figures of her age: an advocate of free love, women's rights, and birth control. Her rhetorical skills even won high praise from George Bernard Shaw. Leon Czolgosz, President McKinley's assassin, claimed to have been inspired by her, causing Emma to be incarcerated for two weeks despite the lack of any evidence linking her to the crime. When Alexander was released from prison in 1906, Emma founded a periodical called Mother Earth, *and remained its editor until it was suppressed in 1917. In 1908, Dr. Benjamin Reitman (a "handsome brute," according to Emma) swept the anarchist off her feet. She wrote him hundreds of letters in which she revealed a far more vulnerable and emotionally dependent persona than popularly believed, and the letter below was written the year their affair began. Their relationship lasted ten years, but collapsed under the weight of his promiscuous, often exploitative nature. Though she adhered to the concept of free love, she could not bear Ben's flirting with other women and she returned to Alexander. In Ben's book* The Second Oldest Profession *(1931), he recounts that Emma "taught me that men and women will never be free until they learn not to exploit or be exploited."*

September 27, 1908

You have opened up the prison gates of my womanhood. And all the passion that was unsatisfied in me for so many years, leaped into a wild reckless storm boundless as the sea . . . Can you then imagine that I could stay away from you? What is love, family ties, the power of association to the wanderer in the desert. His mind is bent on the spring that will quench his thirst . . . Yet, if I were asked to choose between a world of understanding and the spring that fills my body with fire, I should have to choose the spring. It is life, sunshine, music, untold ecstasy. The Spring, oh ye Gods, that have tortured my body all these years, I will give you my soul only let me drink, drink from the Spring of my master lover . . . There. You have the confession of a starved tortured being . . . my Ben.

Emma Goldman

Ronald Reagan to Nancy Reagan

". . . he discovered the joy of loving . . ."

Ronald Reagan (b. 1911). Fortieth president of the United States. Ronald's remarkable charm earned him the sobriquet "The Great Communicator." His off-hand, folksy style was thought by some to be a product of his sportscasting and Hollywood acting days, yet his letters and manuscripts reveal a clear-thinking and straightforward view of life. All presidents "act" the role of president, and perhaps Ronald's film experience helped him perform his role on the world's stage better than many others who held the office. The achievements and failures of his presidency and its legacy are still hotly debated.

Nancy Reagan's (nee Davis) brief career as an actress ended with the 1951 movie Hellcats of the Navy, *where she played opposite her future husband, Ronald. They were married in 1952. The following letter is a tribute to their loving and supportive relationship, now half a century old.*

Nancy and Ronald Reagan

March 4, 1981

Dear First Lady

As Pres. of the U.S., it is my honor & privilege to cite you for service above and beyond the call of duty in that you have made one man (me) the most happy man in the world for 29 years.

Beginning in 1951, Nancy Davis, seeing the plight of a lonely man who didn't know how lonely he really was, determined to rescue him from a completely empty life. Refusing to be rebuffed by a certain amount of stupidity on his part she ignored his somewhat slow response. With patience & tenderness she gradually brought the light of understanding to his darkened obtuse mind and he discovered the joy of loving someone, with all his heart.

Nancy Davis then went on to bring him happiness for the next 29 years as Nancy Davis Reagan for which she has received & will continue to receive his undying devotion forever & ever.

She has done this in spite of the fact that he still can't find the words to tell her how lost he would be without her. He sits in the Oval office from which he can see (if he scrooches down) her window and feels warm all over just knowing she is there.

The above is the statement of the man who benefited from her act of heroism.

The below is his signature.

Ronald Reagan —Pres. of the U.S.

P.S. He—I mean, I love and adore you.

Painful Separations

Dylan Thomas to Caitlin Thomas

"Have you forgotten me?"

Dylan Thomas (1914–1953). Welsh poet and writer. Dylan was a sickly and neurotic child who dropped out of school at age sixteen. He made a name for himself at twenty with the publication of his first book, Eighteen Poems (*1934*). *In 1936, the year* Twenty-Five Poems *was published, he met a young Irishwoman, Caitlin Macnamara, and married her the following year. Lacking any business acumen, and with a growing family to support (the couple had three children), Dylan quickly fell upon hard times. It became increasingly difficult to sustain a happy life, especially under the burden of his heavy drinking problem. After suffering a nervous breakdown in 1947, friends were able to find a cottage for Dylan's family in Wales. In 1950, the first of four lecture tours to the United States was arranged, and Dylan gave numerous and well-attended readings. His letters to Caitlin are often far more* passionate than her responses — she no doubt had a hard life with this exceptionally gifted poet. But long-standing income tax debts, a shaky marriage, and increased drinking contributed to his unhappiness. After an enormous binge in a New York bar, Dylan collapsed and died just a few days after his thirty-ninth birthday.

"I am the man you used to say you loved."

March 16th 1950

Cat: my cat: If only you would write to me: My love, oh cat. This is not, as it seems from the address above, a dive, joint, saloon, etc., but the honourable & dignified headquarters of the dons of the University of Chicago. I love you. That is all I know. But all I know, too, is that I am writing into space: the kind of dreadful, unknown space I am just going to enter. I am going to Iowa, Illinois, Idaho, Indindiana, but these, though misspelt, are on the map. You are not. Have you forgotten me? I am the man you used to say you loved. I used to sleep in your arms—do you remember? But you never write. You are perhaps mindless of me. I am not of you. I love you. There isn't a moment of any hideous day when I do not say to myself, "It will be alright. I shall go home. Caitlin loves me. I love Caitlin." But perhaps you have forgotten. If you have forgotten, or lost your affection for me, please, my Cat, let me know. I Love You.

Franz Kafka to
Felice Bauer

"I am with you once more . . ."

Franz Kafka (1883–1924). German novelist born in Prague, of German-Jewish parents. Kafka's posthumously published novels won him international acclaim through their expression of humanity's anxieties and feelings of alienation. Tormented by his father and their difficult relationship, his story Das Urteil _(The Judgement; 1916), is a depiction of that struggle, which is also reflected in Kafka's problematic love life. There were only a few women whom he loved, and chief among them was Felice Bauer, to whom he was twice engaged. Their final parting came in 1917, the same year he was diagnosed with tuberculosis. In a last desperate effort to escape his parents and concentrate on his writing, Kafka moved to Berlin. His deteriorating health forced him to enter a clinic near Vienna, where he died in 1924. This letter, written in December 1912, dates from the first year of Kafka and_

Felice's relationship and reads like a brief episode from one of his masterworks.

Well dearest, the doors are shut, all is quiet, I am with you once more. How many things does 'to be with you' mean by now? I have not slept all day, and while I duly went about all the afternoon and early evening with a heavy head and a befogged brain, now, as night sets in, I am almost excited, feel within me a tremendous desire to write; the demon inhabiting the writing urge begins to stir at most inopportune moments. Let him, I'll go to bed. But if I could spend Christmas writing and sleeping, dearest, that would be wonderful!

I was after you continuously this afternoon, in vain of course. As a matter of fact not quite in vain, for I constantly kept as close as possible to Frau Friedmann, because after all she was close to you for quite a time, because you say *Du* to each other, and because she happens to be the possessor of letters from you, which I certainly begrudge her. But why doesn't she say a word about you while I keep staring at her lips, ready to pounce on the first word? Have you stopped writing to each other? Perhaps she knows nothing new about you? But how is this possible! And if she knows nothing new, why doesn't she talk about something old? And if she doesn't want to talk about you, why doesn't she at least mention your name, as she used to, when she was around before? But no, she won't; instead, she keeps me hanging about, and we talk about incredibly unimportant things, such as Breslau, coughing, music, scarves, brooches, hairstyles, Italian holidays, sleigh-rides, beaded bags, stiff shirts, cufflinks, Herbert Schottländer, the French language, public baths, showers,

"...for hours on end my head hums with the desire to hear the name Felice."

cooks, Harden, economic conditions, travelling by night, the Palace Hotel, Schreiberhau, hats, the University of Breslau, relatives—in short about everything under the sun, but the only subject that has, unfortunately, some faint association with you consists of a few words about Pyramidos and aspirin; it is cause for wonder why I pursue this subject for so long, and why I enjoy rolling these two words around my tongue. But really, I am not satisfied with this as the sole outcome of an afternoon, because for hours on end my head hums with the desire to hear the name Felice. Finally, by force, I direct the conversation to the railway connection between Berlin and Breslau, at the same time giving her a menacing look—nothing.

Franz

Napoléon Bonaparte
to Joséphine Bonaparte

"... far from all that I love!"

Napoléon Bonaparte (1769–1821). French military leader and Emperor of France. On March 9, 1796, Napoléon married Marie-Joséphine-Rose Tascher de la Pagerie (1763–1814), widow of the Vicomte de Beauharnais, a general guillotined during the Revolution. At the time of the marriage ceremony, Napoléon overstated his age by two years, and Joséphine understated hers by four, achieving a symbolic balance that was not evident in their future relationship. Two days later, he departed to take command of the Army of Italy. His feelings about Joséphine, however, were deeply passionate, as reflected in this letter from Italy, written two months after his departure, and just three days after the Battle of Lodi. For Joséphine, however, the relationship was character-ized by affection rather than passion, and she engaged in a number of affairs, which nearly caused Napoléon to divorce her in October 1799. By falsely suggesting that she was pregnant, Joséphine was able to temporarily hide her affairs and postpone a separation. Unable to produce a male heir, Napoléon finally divorced her in order to marry the Archduchess Marie-Louise of Austria. A son was born in 1811, and Napoléon immediately proclaimed him the King of Rome. Joséphine's letters to Napoléon have not survived, but a number of his remain. They were found buried in a closet in her home, Malmaison, by a valet, and subsequently sold and dispersed. Although Napoléon may have intentionally destroyed her letters, she was never far from his thoughts. On his deathbed, his last words were: "France! . . . Army! . . . Head of the Army! . . . Joséphine!"

"Things are going well here; but my heart is indescribably heavy. You are ill and far away from me."

So it is true that you are pregnant. Murat has written to me; but he tells me it is making you ill and that he thinks it is unwise for you to undertake so long a journey. So I must still be deprived of the joy of holding you in my arms! I must still spend several months far from all that I love! Is it possible that I shan't have the pleasure of seeing you with your little belly? That should make you interesting! You write that you have changed. Your letter is short and sad and shakily written. What is it, my adorable? What can be upsetting you? Oh! Don't stay in the country; go to town, try to assume yourself and remember that there is no truer torment for my soul than to know you unwell and unhappy. I thought I was jealous, but I swear to you that I am not. I think I would rather myself give you a lover than know you to be miserable. So be gay and cheerful, and remember that my happiness depends on yours. If Joséphine is unhappy, if she lets herself be sad and discouraged, then she doesn't love me. Soon you are going to bring into the world another being who will love you as much as I—No, that is impossible, but your children and I will always be around you to convince you of our love and care. You won't be horrid, will you? No tantrums!!! Except as a joke. And then just two or three pouts; nothing is prettier, and a little kiss puts everything right.

The courier has brought your letter of the 18th. How sad it makes me! Can't you be happy, darling Joséphine? Is there something you want? I am waiting impatiently for Murat to know all the details of what you are doing, what you are saying, whom you are seeing, what you are wearing. Everything to do with my adorable is dear to my heart, which only longs to know.

Things are going well here; but my heart is indescribably heavy. You are ill and far away from me. Be gay and take great care of yourself, you who are worth more than all the universe to me. The thought that you are ill makes me very unhappy . . .

George Sand to
Gustave Flaubert

"We love you, sad or cheerful."

George Sand (1804–1876). French romantic novelist. George Sand was the pseudonym of Amandine Aurore Lucie Dudevant (nee Dupin). This letter was written on September 7, 1875, to the author of Madame Bovary *(1857), French novelist Gustave Flaubert (1821–1880).*

You're upset and depressed, and you make me upset too. Never mind—I'd rather have you complain than keep silent, dear friend, and I don't want you to stop writing me. I have great sorrows too, and often. My old friends are dying before me. One of the dearest, who brought Maurice up and on whom I was counting to help me bring up my granddaughters, has just died quite suddenly. It's a great grief to me. Life is a series of blows. But there's no getting away from duty: we must just go on and do what we have to do without saddening those who suffer when we do. I beg you to exercise your will, and not to forget we share in your distress. Tell us that things are more peaceful and that the outlook is brighter. We love you, sad or cheerful. Write and tell us how things go.

Although they first met in 1859, Sand and Flaubert's intense friendship commenced in 1863 when she wrote an article praising Gustave's otherwise poorly received novel Salammbô *(1862). With this short, yet typically sympathetic letter, Sand hoped to encourage the younger Flaubert, who three weeks earlier had written to her, "I long to die as soon as possible, because I am finished, emptied out, and older than if I were a hundred . . . I no longer have Faith. And work of any kind has become impossible for me." Yet, by early October, Flaubert had taken steps to bolster his morale and planned a new story based on the legend of Saint Julian the Hospitaller. It was precisely these types of relationships, ones that aroused Sand's compassion, which were to have significance in her life. She once confided to her friend, Juliette La Massine, "As I examine myself, I can see that the only real passions of my life were maternity and friendship." Her relationship with Flaubert deeply touched, perhaps, both aspects. As she herself notes, the seventy-one-year old Sand was still grieving over the death of Jules Boucoiran, her son Maurice's former tutor, who had died at Nimes on August 18. Nine months later, she passed away, leaving Flaubert to observe, "She will remain one of the radiant splendors of France, unequaled in her glory."*

*Abigail Smith to
John Adams*

"Friendship is a band yet stronger"

*Abigail Smith (1744–1818). Wife of President John Adams
(1735–1826), and mother of the sixth president, John Quincy Adams.
Abigail was a "modern woman" in the old-fashioned sense. Though separated from her husband for nearly half their marriage due to the
demands of John's political life, and ladened with the largely solitary task
of raising four children while managing her husband's affairs, she was an
especially bright, articulate, and politically astute individual. Despite her
often lengthy absences from Washington, her influence on her husband
was significant. Recognized even in her lifetime as a brilliant letter
writer, Abigail declined to have any of her missives published. One of her
most famous notes is the so-called "Remember the Ladies" letter. In it,
among other things, she urges that women are entitled to share in the
fruits of liberty, including a married woman's right to own property.*

This lovely example, using the pseudonym "Diana," was sent to her future husband a little more than a year before their marriage.

My Friend   Weymouth August th 11 1763

If I was sure your absence today was occasioned, by what it generally is, either to wait upon Company, or promote some good work, I freely confess my Mind would be much more at ease than at present it is. Yet this uneasiness does not arise from any apprehension of Slight or neglect, but a fear least you are indisposed, for that you said should be your only hindrance.

Humanity obliges us to be affected with the distresses and Miserys of our fellow creatures. Friendship is a band yet stronger, which causes us to [fee]l with greater tenderness the afflictions of our Friends.

And there is a tye more binding than Humanity, and stronger than Friendship, which makes us anxious for the happiness and welfare of those to whom it binds us. It makes their Misfortunes, Sorrows and afflictions, our own. Unite these, and there is a threefold cord—by this cord I am not ashamed to own myself bound, nor do I [believe] that you are wholly free from it. Judg [e you then] for your Diana has she not this day [had sufficien]t cause for pain and anxiety of mind?

Adieu may this find you in better health than I fear it will, and happy as your Diana wishes you.

Accept this hasty Scrawl warm from the Heart of Your Sincere

Diana

Abigail and John Adams

*"And there is a tye...
which makes us anxious
for the happiness and
welfare of those to
whom it binds us."*

My Friend   Weymonth August the 11
                              If I was Sure your absence to day
was occasioned, by what it generally is, either to wait upon
Company, or promote some good work, I freely confess
my Mind would be much more at ease than at present it
is — yet this uneasiness does not arise from any apprehension of Slight or neglect, but a fear least you are indisposed for that you Said should be your only hindrance.
                              Humanity obliges us to be af-
fected with the distresses and Misferys of our fellow creatures
friendship is a band yet Stronger, which causes us to
feel with greater tenderness the afflictions of our friends.
                              And there is a tye more binding than Humani-
ty, and Stronger than friendship, which makes us
anxious for the happiness and welfare of those to whom
it binds us. it makes their [   ]tunes Sorrows and
affliction our own [   ]te these, and there is
a threefold cord — by [   ] not ashamed to own
my self bound, nor do [   ] you are wholly
free from it — judg[   ] or your Diana
has she not that [   ] use for pain
and anxiety of mind [   ]
                              She bids [   ] that Seneca for
the Sake of his Paulina [   ]ful and tender of
his health, the health and happiness of Seneca she says
was not dearer to his Paulina, than that of Lysander
to his Diana
                              The fabrick often wants

Simone de Beauvoir to Nelson Algren

"Anyway, now it is here, it is love, and my heart aches."

Simone de Beauvoir (1908–1986). French existentialist writer, novelist, and feminist. Simone studied philosophy with Jean-Paul Sartre in 1929 at the Sorbonne, and remained his companion until his death in 1980. Her own works reflect existentialist views combined with a feminine sensibility, notably in her most famous piece Le Deuxième Sexe *(*The Second Sex, 1949*) and her masterpiece* Les Mandarins *(*The Mandarins, 1954*). In 1947, Simone first met American writer Nelson Algren (1909–1981), author of* The Man with the Golden Arm *(1949) and* A Walk on the Wild Side *(1956) in Chicago during a trip to the United States. Despite their cultural and philosophical differences, their transatlantic romance was torrid and enduring, lasting for more than seventeen years. This letter to her "precious, beloved Chicago man," is* *part of an archive recently acquired by Ohio State University, and was written the day she returned to Paris after their first meeting in America.*

Sunday, 18 Mai 1947

My Precious beloved Chicago man,

I think of you in Paris, in Paris I miss you. The whole journey was marvellous. We had nearly no night since we went to the East. At Newfoundland the sun began to set, but five hours later it was rising in Shannon, above a sweet green Irish landscape. Everything was so beautiful and I had so much to think that I hardly slept. This morning at 10 (it was 6 by your time), I was in the heart of Paris. I hoped the beauty of Paris would help me to get over my sadness; but it did not. First, Paris is not beautiful today. It is grey and cloudy; it is Sunday, the streets

"My heart is yet in New York, at the corner of Broadway where we said goodbye..."

are empty, and everything seems dull, dark, and dead. Maybe it is my heart which is dead to Paris. My heart is yet in New York, at the corner of Broadway where we said goodbye; it is in my Chicago home, in my own warm place against your loving heart. I suppose in two or three days it will be a bit different. I must be concerned again by all the French intellectual and politic life, by my work and my friends. But today I don't even whish to get interested in all these things; I feel lazzy and tired, and I can enjoy only memories. My beloved one, I don't know why I waited so long before saying I loved you. I just wanted to be *sure* and not to say easy, empty words. But it seems to me now love was there since the beginning. Anyway, now it is here, it is love and my heart aches. I am happy to be so bitterly unhappy because I know you are unhappy, too, and it is sweet to have a part of the same sadness. With you pleasure was love, and now pain is love too. We must know every kind of love. We'll know the joy of meeting again. I want it, I need it, and I'll get it. Wait for me. I wait for you. I love you more even than I said, more maybe than you know. I'll write very often. Write to me very often too. I am your wife forever.

Your Simone

I read the whole book and I like it *very* much. I'll have it translated, sure. Kisses and kisses and kisses. It was so sweet when you kissed me. I love you.

Mary Todd Lincoln to Harriet Wilson

"... my deeply afflicted heart ..."

Mary Todd Lincoln (1818–1882). Wife of President Abraham Lincoln, whom she married in 1842. Possessed of a somewhat immature, but vivacious personality, she was characterized shortly before her marriage to Lincoln as "the very creature of excitement." Lincoln's more expansive, yet dour personality no doubt found room for, and even pleasure in, Mary's high-strung ways. Her years as First Lady were difficult—accused of overspending, exorbitant White House entertaining, and even Southern sympathies, her life began, inexorably, to fall apart after the death of a son, Edward, in 1850. Following the death of the couple's favorite child, Willie, in 1862, and her husband's assassination in April 1865, Mary was never to know happiness again. She lived another seventeen years in sorrow, further complicated by the death a third son, Tad, in 1871, and a brief institutionalization arranged by her last remaining child, Robert, in 1875.

This letter from June 8, 1865, written less than two months after her hus-band's murder, to her friend, Harriet Malvina Wilson, wife of Senator Henry Wilson of Massachusetts, underscores Mary and her children's over-whelming despair.

Your very kind and totally truly sympathizing letter, was received a few days since, pray, receive the grateful thanks of my deeply afflicted heart, for the words of affection & comfort it contained. My precious Boys and myself, are left very desolate & broken hearted, the deep waters of affliction have almost overwhelmed us and we find it very difficult, to bow in submission, to our Heavenly Father's will, the light of our life, has been taken away. I shall always feel most grateful, to your Noble Husband, for his unwavering friendship & faithful support of the President, which was highly appreciated, I assure you, by his grateful heart. I had truly hoped, in the coming four years, we had anticipated residing in Washington, that circumstances would have drawn you and myself together, and I should have been privileged to number you, with my cherished friends. Our Heavenly Father, has so disposed events has removed my idolized Husband, from me, my Boys, are deprived of their counselor & protector, my all, & the one, so devoted always to me, is removed from our sight forever! The knowledge that my sons, depend upon me, for their comfort & happiness, alone, prevents me, from pleading, with our gracious Saviour, to remove me, from a world, in which, we have been called upon, to suffer so much. In our griefs, we are said to be selfish, I hope you will excuse my sending you so lengthy a letter . . .

Radclyffe Hall to Evguenia Souline

"I feel battle-weary, and you are my rest, my joy . . ."

Marguerite Radclyffe Hall (1886–1943). English writer and author of the 1928 landmark novel, The Well of Loneliness, *considered to be the earliest literary exploration of lesbianism. Though banned in Britain, it was quickly published in France, and enjoyed such success that it was translated into eleven languages and sold more than one million copies during the author's lifetime. Born into a wealthy family, Radclyffe was educated at Queens College in London and, upon graduating, inherited her father's fortune. With short hair and a propensity for men's clothing and cigars, she abandoned her Christian name in favor of "Radclyffe," and to those who knew her well, "John." While on holiday in Germany in 1907, Radclyffe met her first love, a beautiful Edwardian socialite named Mabel Batten, who encouraged Radclyffe to publish her work. Although*

Mabel was twelve years her senior, the two lived together until Mabel's death in 1916. However, shortly before her death, Radclyffe met and began a relationship with Mabel's cousin Uta Troubridge. Late in life she fell in love with Evguenia Souline, a Russian-born nurse hired to care for Uta, when she was temporarily ill. The following letter is written to Evguenia. Uta cared for Radclyffe until her death from cancer in 1943 and arranged for her burial in Highgate Cemetery alongside Mabel.

"It seems so strange and so terribly wrong not to be able to talk to you... Last night I had one of my fits of the glooms."

November 26, 1934

Beloved . . . No letter from you today as yet—this is because there has been a Sunday—I am growing to dread the weekends . . . It seems so strange and so terribly wrong not to be able to talk to you, not to be able to discuss things together . . . Last night I had one of my fits of the glooms. When the weight of life lay heavy upon me, when everything seemed dust and ashes in my mouth, when I felt that I had not made good at all, that I never would make good being what I am—that the scales were too heavily weighted against me—I get like this sometimes and have done for years—it is the melancholy of the inverted. I tell you this because it is God's truth that you can lift me right out of such moods, that when I am lying in your arms and you in mine such moods cannot touch me, that you, Soulina, can make me forget the great weariness of spirit, mind & body that I feel sometimes—I feel battle-weary, and you are my rest, my joy, and my ultimate justification. When I am with you I am younger than you are, I am young and carefree and irresponsible in nearly all things save your happiness; I am back where I was many years ago with only one difference—I know that I am kinder & more considerate & understanding. Oh, well, it may be that I should be glad that life has knocked me about a bit if because of this it has made John a more worthy & steadfast love for Soulina. Dearest I must stop . . . God bless you my rest, my joy and my hope . . . Your John

Fire

and

Ice

Anaïs Nin to Henry Miller

"your letters now sound . . . cold, egotistical . . ."

Anaïs Nin (1903–1977). French-born author of novels and short sto-ries. Her reputation is based largely on eight published volumes of diaries and her influence on the Surrealist movement. After her father, Spanish composer Joaquin Nin, abandoned his family, Anaïs and her mother sailed to New York in 1914. She briefly attended school, and then quit in order to work as a model and study dance. In 1923, Anaïs married Hugh Guiler, a New York banker, and moved back to Paris the following year. Financially comfortable, she and her husband were able to support sev-eral avant-garde artists, notably the American writer Henry Miller (1891–1980) who moved to Paris in 1930. His literary association with Anaïs turned into a torrid affair that reached a bizarre climax when Henry's actress wife, June Mansfield, visited Paris in 1931. Henry introduced her to Anaïs, and the two women instantly fell in love with each other. In 1941, after returning to the United States from Greece, where he had gone to visit Lawrence Durrell (also one of Nin's lovers), Henry wrote her insisting that she join him in California. The following is her response.

Anaïs Nin

You can do whatever pleases you, but your letters now sound exactly like the letters you sent me from Greece, which almost estranged us for good. They are cold, egotistical and concerned purely with pleasure. All you can answer to my emotional attitude when I think I can leave and then cannot leave is thoroughly inhuman and mechanical . . . Everything would be all right if you wrote the right kind of letters. But you write the worst letters, letters bad enough to estrange anyone. I have never seen more expressionless, pan-faced letters, in regard to whether I come or do not come etc. More self-centered letters either. That's what creates distance, not time or a trip. The real distance and separation were always created by your letters.

Voltaire to Marie Louise Denis

"A thousand kisses, my dear . . ."

Voltaire (pseudonym for François Marie Arouet; 1694–1778). French philosopher and writer; author of the celebrated Candide *(1759), and justly considered the embodiment of eighteenth-century Enlightenment. Voltaire had three great loves in his life: Madame Emile du Châtelet, his niece Madame Marie Louise Denis, and an unquenchable thirst for knowledge. A man of enormous genius and talent, Voltaire not only knew many of the great minds and monarchs of Europe, but exercised enormous intellectual influence over them as well. His books and essays, particularly the notable* Lettres Philosophiques *(1734), are considered ground-breaking works in the history of modern thought. Curiously,* Lettres Philosophiques, *with its anti-religious ideas, precipitated his first love affair. Because of the inflamatory nature of his work, a warrant had been issued for Voltaire's arrest, and he took refuge at the home of Madame du Châtelet at Cirey in Champagne.*

Madame du Châtelet was a brilliant woman who shared, and even modestly influenced, some of her lover's works. While still involved with her, Voltaire established a liaison with his recently widowed niece, Madame Denis; a relationship, which although it would not have necessarily been frowned upon, he initially kept secret. His letters to her are written in Italian to further disguise their affair. In the meantime, Madame du Châtelet had fallen in love with a poet, but sadly died in childbirth, with Voltaire, her lover of fifteen years, at her side. He spent the next twenty-nine years in the company of his beloved niece, Madame Denis, to whom this letter is written.

So it is today that I shall see you, today that I shall regain the only consolation that can assuage the bitterness of my life. Nature, which bestowed on me the tenderest of hearts, forgot to give me a stomach. I cannot digest, but I can love. I love you, and will love you until the day of my death. A thousand kisses, my dear virtuosa. You write Italian much better than I. You deserve to be admitted to the academy of the Crusca.

My heart and my cazzo greet you most tenderly. I shall certainly see you this evening.

(Madame Denis crossed out the word "cazzo," a vulgar reference to the penis, and replaced it with "spirito!")

"I'm blaming the ages of women who have gone before you . . ."

James Thurber (1894–1961). American humorist and cartoonist. Thurber wrote short stories and drew witty cartoons as a staff member of The New Yorker, *which he joined in 1927. The same issues he so adroitly and humorously wrote about in* Is Sex Necessary? *(1929) and* The Secret Life of Walter Mitty *(1942), he seems to have faced with Eva Prout, the recipient of this letter from the spring of 1920.*

So my letter was sarcastic. Do you think it is a simple matter to give one's whole heart away, his whole being, his entire self, to a girl who may be a little amused, somewhat pleased, and only on occasions seriously realizing what she has had given to her.

A woman is often a wonderful thing. And you are. But in you, as in all of them, is the indifference of Carmen, the joy in cruelty of Cleopatra, the tyrannical marble-heartedness of Katherine de Medici, and the cold glitter of all the passionless despots of men's warm souls since sex first originated—since Eve broke the heart of humanity forever and laughed with sadistic joy at Adam sweating blood on the rack she made for him . . .

I'm not blaming you. I'm blaming the ages of women gone before you who handed such legacies down, blaming the radiant and sparkling and fidgety ladies of history who kissed in a moment of coquetry and saw men die, kings dethroned and nations fight in blood because of that careless caress. Men are fools, weak, wine-blooded, deeply-devoted darn fools. What have women done for them half so intense and potent as what they have done to them? Whom the gods destroy they first make madly in love with a girl.

George Bernard Shaw to Stella Campbell

"Bah! You have no nerve: you have no brain . . ."

George Bernard Shaw (1856–1950). Irish playwright, essayist, music critic, and socialist; winner of the Nobel Prize for Literature in 1925. Though Shaw did not have a very publicized love life (he remained loyal to his wife Charlotte), he was extraordinarily passionate about the actress Mrs. Patrick Campbell, known as Stella. They maintained a correspondence that spanned forty years, beginning when Shaw was forty-two and not an especially well-known playwright, and Stella was thirty-four, at the height of her career. Though she inspired Shaw to write Pygmalion *(an idea he had for her as early as 1897), she steadfastly refused to play the lead, Eliza Doolittle. When she relented, it became, arguably, the greatest success of her career. Over time, Shaw's plays grew increasingly popular while Stella performed less and less, until she half-heartedly attempted to forge a career in Hollywood.*

And what of his wife? Charlotte endured the hardship of Shaw's parallel affections. In a 1933 letter from Alexander Woollcott to Thornton Wilder, he noted, "Did Ruth [Gordon] ever tell you of that luncheon in our villa when Shaw talked about Stella Campbell for an hour and a half until Mrs. Shaw was driven to beating a tattoo with her salad fork as a way of warning him that she couldn't stand another word on the subject?" Stella broke Shaw's heart, perhaps just momentarily, when she decided to marry George Cornwallis West. He was not pleased as he declares in this vitriolic letter from August 11, 1913, the second of three missives he sent to her that day.

Very well, go: the loss of a woman is not the end of the world. The sun shines on: it is pleasant to swim: it is good to work: my soul can stand alone. But I am deeply, deeply, deeply wounded. You have tried me; and you are not comfortable with me: I cannot bring you to peace, or rest, or even fun: there is nothing really frank in our comradeship after all. It is I who have been happy, carelessly happy, comfortable, able to walk for miles after dinner at top speed in search of you, singing all the way (I had walked eight miles in the morning, by the way, and written a scene in my play) and to become healthily and humorously sleepy afterwards the moment I saw that you were rather bored and that the wind was in the wrong quarter. Bah! You have no nerve: you have no brain: you are the caricature of an eighteenth century male sentimentalist, a Hedda Gabler titivated with odds and ends from Burne Jones's ragbag: you know nothing, God help you, except what you know all wrong: daylight blinds you: you run after life furtively and run away or

"Very well, go: the loss of a woman is not the end of the world."

huddle up and scream when it turns and opens its arms to you: you are a man's disgrace and infatuation not his crown "above rubies" instead of adding the world to yourself you detach yourself, extricate yourself, guard yourself: instead of a thousand charms for a thousand different people you have one fascination with which you blunder about—hit or miss—with old and young, servants, children, artists, Philistines: you are a one-part actress and that one not a real part: you are an owl, sickened by two days of my sunshine: I have treated you far too well, idolized, thrown my heart and mind to you (as I throw them to all the world) to make what you could of; and what you make of them is to run away. Go then: the Shavian oxygen burns up your little lungs: seek some stuffiness that suits you. You will not marry George! At the last moment you will funk him or be ousted by a bolder soul. You have wounded my vanity: an inconceivable audacity, an unpardonable crime. Farewell, wretch that I loved.

Her response two days later is worth noting:

You vagabond you—you blind man. You weaver of words, you—and black and purple winged hider of cherubs—you poor thing unable to understand a mere woman . . . No daughters to relieve your cravings—no babes to stop your satirical chatterings, why should I pay for all your shortcomings. You in your broom-stick and sheet have crackers and ashes within you. I in my rags and my trimmings have a little silver lamp in my soul and to keep its flame burning is all that I ask. That I pray. My friend—my dear friend all the same.

Sarah Bernhardt to Jean Richepin

"... trample me under your storms ..."

Sarah Bernhardt (born Henriette Rosine Bernard; 1844–1923). French actress. Born in Paris, Sarah was the illegitimate child of mixed French-Dutch parentage of Jewish descent. She entered the Paris Conservatoire in 1859, winning fame in 1867 as Zanetto in Coppée's Le Passant *and the Queen of Spain in* Ruy Blas. *After 1876, she frequently appeared on stage in London, the United States, and Europe. In 1882, she married Jacques Damala, a Greek actor possessed of limited talent and an over-sized ego, from whom she later separated. Among her lovers were the Belgian Prince de Ligne (by whom she had her only child, Maurice), the artist Gustave Doré, numerous actors, and the picaresque French poet, dramatist, and novelist Jean Richepin (1849–1926). This turbulent and torturous affair began shortly after her husband left to serve in the army in North Africa. A short time later, Jacques returned, bringing home gambling debts and a new mistress. Sarah took him back, threw*

Jean out, then threw Jacques out, and carried on in much the same dra-
matic manner as she performed on stage. However, as evinced in the fol-
lowing letter, there can be no doubt that she was deeply in love with Jean.

Sarah Bernhardt

My adulated one, my distracting master, I beg your pardon.
Oh, do forgive me! Did I say so many bad and infamous things
then that you had to write such angry words? I feel dizzy under
the torrent of your anger; your phrases stab my heart and carve
themselves into my being. I have read eight phrases of your letter
and they were all struggling to be the first to arrive. I am tired of
your continual scolding and I am still yours more than ever—the
blame is yours; I cannot be distant from you . . .

Come back! I implore you, come back—tomorrow I will
write you an official letter telling you to come back quick,
quick! See, Jean, truly I cannot help it. I adore you; I am all
yours because it had to be, because that's how I feel for you.
My letter could reach you only now because you were not free.
It is not my fault—I wrote one ten days ago saying that I love

you as I do today; I swear I am incapable of betraying you. Yes, I know too well that I like being a traitor, that I am made of bad thoughts and treason—I am everything it pleases you to call me. I have been all these things; the superiority I felt over all those around me created my perversity; but that is all dead, nothing exists anymore. You came—you breathed your powerful breath over me and other people, my hesitations, and my whys and wherefores all crumbled. I drank on your lips the truth of love and I trembled in your arms, feeling the real, mad sensation of bodily rapture, and I saw in your eyes the absolute superiority of your being. With the beauty of a new flower I gave myself completely for I brought you a being that belonged only to you. I invented nothing about me, I felt it all afresh.

So you see, Jean, you must forgive my bad temper. As soon as you left, it overwhelmed me, leaving me no time for reflection. Still moist from your arms, perfumed by your being, it showed me the bed, the night, the awakening, the kiss, the loving . . . All right, all right! Let's not talk of my temper any more. I beg you to forgive me for all I may have asked you. With both my arms around your neck I ask you to forgive me—I'm sick of having shouted so loudly.

There, be kind; take me close to you, my Jean. Sing me some of your beautiful verses, bear me away in tender blue leaves, roll me over in dark clouds, trample me under your storms, break me in your rage, but love me well. My adored lover, love me in the name of love.

My claws are strong but they cannot leave a lasting mark in your heart if you run away from me. Tell me that it's all finished, that you'll destroy that stupid letter—but most of all tell me that you know I'm faithful, that I can't betray you: it would be cowardly, infamous and stupidly foolish.

My letter was a cry of vengeance and you believed in it. Still, you must know it was only a scream of rage and real anguish. But don't you know, adored Master, that you are always near me, looking at me with your golden clarity; don't you know that my hand ceaselessly brushes against yours, that I find myself talking to you, offering my lips: this is the spell I'm suffering under. How can you suspect me of planning only for the moment, of stealing a parcel of what belongs to you? . . . You would notice such a theft, I'm sure, and I feel ashamed just thinking about it—quiet, calm yourself. From high above, very high, very high, where you shall be, pity my confused folly. I was hurt, I was wary—Everything you do must be and is right. I submit myself to your will and I subdue my pride: you shall punish me by refusing me your lips for a second . . .

Tell me that your faith in me revives, though all your hopes are ragged. Let us begin our flight again and even though you make me suffer too much I won't stop our mad race. I shall hurl myself down from above, my love, I shall nod to you and kill myself in the fall.

⚹ I kiss each of your hairs, gently I calm your adored body and my lips ask a hundred thousand pardons and beg that your lips be given back to me.

Sarah's on-again, off-again, relationship with Jacques was too much for Richepin to bear, and he finally warned the frivolous and drug-addicted actor that the world was simply not big enough for the two of them. Jacques retreated, and Jean confidently claimed Sarah as his own. But the great actress belonged to no one, and she continued her affairs, thereby alienating Jean as a lover, but retaining him as a friend until her death, forty years later.

Marcel Proust to

Daniel Halévy

"You think me jaded and effete."

Marcel Proust (1871–1922). French novelist and author of the monumental Remembrance of Things Past *(1912). The death of his father in 1903 and mother in 1905 left Proust emotionally devastated but financially well off. He withdrew from society, lived in a soundproof apartment, and gave himself over entirely to introspection and writing. In 1912, he produced the first part of his thirteen-volume masterpiece,* À la Recherche du Temps Perdu *(*Remembrance of Things Past*), a work that has earned him an international reputation that endures to this day. This massive novel, exploring the power of memory and the unconscious, as well as the nature of writing itself, has had a profound influence on psychology and literature. This youthful letter was written around the fall of 1888 to Daniel Halévy (1872–1962), Proust's schoolmate.*

You gave me quite a little thrashing, but your switches are so flowery that I can't be angry with you and the fragrance of those flowers has intoxicated me enough to soften the harshness of the thorns. You have beaten me with a lyre. Your lyre is delightful . . . I will tell you what I think, or rather chat with you as one chats with an exquisite boy about things quite worthy of interest, even if one is reluctant to speak of them. I hope you will be grateful to me for my delicacy. To me indelicacy is an abomination. Much worse than debauchery. My ethical beliefs allow me to respect certain feelings, a certain refinement in friendship, and especially the French language, an amiable and infinitely gracious lady, whose sadness and delight are equally exquisite, but upon whom one must never impose obscene poses. That would be to dishonor her beauty.

You think me jaded and effete. You are mistaken. If you are delicious, if you have lovely eyes which reflect the grace and refinement of your mind with such purity that I feel I cannot fully love your mind without kissing your eyes, if your body and mind, like your thoughts, are so lithe and slender that I feel I could mingle more intimately with your thoughts by sitting on your lap, if, finally, I feel that the charm of your person, in which I cannot separate your keen mind from your agile body, would refine and enhance 'the sweet joy of love' for me, there is nothing in all that to deserve your contemptuous words, which would have been more fittingly addressed to someone surfeited with women and seeking new pleasures in pederasty. I am glad to say that I have some highly intelligent friends, distinguished by great moral delicacy, who have amused them-

"They held that these at once sensual and intellectual friendships are better . . . than affairs with stupid, corrupt women."

selves at one time with a boy . . . That was the beginning of their youth. Later on they went back to women. If that were the ultimate end, what, good God, would they be, and what do you think I am, or more especially shall be, if I have already purely and simply finished with love! I would like to speak to you of two masters of consummate wisdom, who in all their lives plucked only the bloom, Socrates and Montaigne. They permit men in their earliest youth to 'amuse themselves,' so as to know something of all pleasures, and so as to release their excess tenderness. They held that these at once sensual and intellectual friendships are better for a young man with a keen sense of beauty and awakened 'senses' as well, than affairs with stupid, corrupt women. I believe those old Masters were mistaken, and will tell you why. I accept only the general tenor of their advice. Don't call me a pederast, it hurts my feelings. If only for the sake of elegance, I try to remain morally pure . . .

Frank Lloyd Wright to Maude Miriam Noel

"Whatever there was in me for you is absolutely dead—even anger."

Frank Lloyd Wright (1867–1959). American architect and theorist. Known for his strikingly original designs, including New York's Guggenheim Museum and the weekend retreat Fallingwater, Wright is America's most influential architect. Minimally trained as an engineer, he learned his trade as an apprentice to Chicago architects, J. L. Silsbee and the firm of Dankmar Adler and Louis Sullivan. Soon after his marriage to Catherine Tobin in 1889, he struck out on his own—the size of his firm increasing with the size of his family. His determination to create a Midwestern school of architecture made him the leading innovator in the Prairie style, and work poured into his studio.

Frank Lloyd Wright

"I think there is nothing you can say to me to change what has already taken place. I have nothing to say."

Despite a larger-than-life reputation, his commissions all but disappeared after he left his wife and began an affair with Mamah Cheney Borthwick, the wife of one of his clients. The ensuing damage to his honor and income made Wright forever wary of scandal, yet there seemed to be no refuge for him.

Undeterred from practicing architecture, Wright began work on his own residence and studio, the famous Taliesin. Though few commissions came in, they were significant and his work notable. In 1913, he was dealt a tragic blow when Borthwick, her children, and several workers were murdered and Taliesin set on fire by a deranged employee. Though stunned and forever fearful of fire, Frank rebuilt Taliesin and soon entered into a relationship with sculptor Maude Miriam Noel (1869–1930), the recipient of this letter. Despite their stormy relationship, it endured for over a decade, and included living together in Japan *for five years while Wright worked on Tokyo's Imperial Hotel. Catherine Tobin finally granted Wright a divorce, and he married Noel in 1923. But after only six months, she left him. As with his first marriage, a divorce from Noel could not be obtained quickly enough. Olgivanna Hinzenberg, whom Wright would marry in 1928, was already pregnant by the time he filed for divorce from Noel.*

Got here and called you at 2:30. Got word you had gone to Matinee to return at 4:30. Since 4:30 I have waited here about one hour—to keep the appointment as promised. I think there is nothing you can say to me to change what has already taken place. I have nothing to say. Whatever there was in me for you is absolutely dead—even anger. If you wish to befoul the affair I can not help it. It is necessary for me to look after some work that I neglected, to come here and I can wait no longer. If you have anything to say to me that will affect an amicable separation of our affair you may write to Taliesin. If not I will take the initiative. I will return there early in the week.

Anne Sexton to

Philip Legler

"... work out your constant need for affection ... take the pills and start on the road to growing ..."

Anne Sexton (1928–1974). American poet known for her revealing poems of confessional intensity. Anne eloped before her twentieth birthday and gave birth to two children in quick succession. The victim of postpartum depression, each birth was followed by a nervous breakdown, and, after her second collapse, she made the first of several suicide attempts. As part of her treatment, her psychiatrist suggested that she cultivate her poetic gifts as a way to work out her emotional difficulties. Anne studied with poets Robert Lowell and W. D. Snodgrass, and her mental illness inspired her first book of poetry, To Bedlam and Part Way Back _(1960). She was awarded the Pulitzer Prize in 1966 for_ Live or Die. _This letter is to Philip Legler, an admirer of Anne's work, who_ first met the poet while a member of the English department at Sweet Briar College in Virginia. Both were married when they began an epistolary romance. Several years later, they became lovers, but their relationship led them into a downward spiral of codependence. After Philip left Anne, she tried to kill herself but was unsuccessful. Anne divorced her husband in 1974 and committed suicide the same year.

" *You're sick.*
You need help..."

Seriously, Phil baby, everyone is wrong here. Your love, your abundance for me is partly sick. I can tell you this because I am the healthiest, wisest sickest human you'll meet outside the nut house (patient or doctor/nurse). The sanest thing in the world is love. And what is important is honesty . . . I feel in my heart that if you concentrate (as you have been doing) on your Anne Sexton campaign that you'll run off into a tornado . . . You're sick. You need help . . .

First, foremost, Phil, work out your constant need for affection, closeness with students, or with this poet . . . Phil, take the pills and start on the road to growing . . .

Anne Sexton

Forbidden Love

Louise and Rachel Russell
to Arthur Sullivan

"... love must almost be a blind passion."

Arthur Sullivan (1842–1900). English composer and conductor who collaborated with W. S. Gilbert in writing many of England's most famous operettas, including H.M.S. Pinafore, Iolanthe, *and* The Mikado. *A success by his early twenties, Arthur was a devotee of gambling, horseracing, and society functions. In the late 1860s, he carried on an affair with two daughters of a prominent naval architect. He was unofficially engaged to Rachel Russell, twenty-three, but courted her older sister, Louise. Rachel, who often signed her letters, "Fond Dove," had her name incorporated into Sullivan's song, "O Fair Dove! O Fond Dove!" (1868). The first letter is from Rachel, the next two, from Louise.*

Letter #1

My sweet one,

Your letter made me a little sad for it showed me that your love could not stand the test of absence, & that only physical contact could re-create it into what it was. Ah me! when I think of those days when cooing and purring was enough for us—till we tried the utmost—& that is why I fancy marriage spoils love. When you can drink brandy water tastes sickly afterwards & so I feel that mere petting & cooing will have no charm for us anymore, & that when we satisfy our passion—then all those little endearments will cease to have any charm. Do you not fear that too, darling, & that is the reason why marriages get so commonplace, that people see & have so much of each other morally & physically that they get satiated, & the freshness of the charm & attraction wears off. Darling why are you not coming today? Because you had enough of me yesterday, I am quietly contented to wait till another opportunity occurs? When will you come again—don't you want to see me darling, or can you wait patiently? Where shall I turn as your love gets cold. It is not the same thing as it was when you saw me daily constantly & I feel as if my heart would break if your love grew cold. There are no more the same endearments or caresses & tendernesses—if it is not passion it is nothing—& I do so fear I have given myself to you too completely. You no longer care to see me or be with me unless you can give way to that completely. Is it not so Arthur, my own love? And your letters are so short & so different to the long love letters I used to get—I feel inclined to say "Take me mother earth. I have loved & been beloved" but I don't want ever to waken from my dream except in heaven. I am sure you will be kind & tender & affectionate to me, as you are to everything you . . . come across & that you live with. But I must have my ideal or—nothing. The ideal we have dreamed together in the old days when we walked in the moonlight—long ago. Don't give me stones when I ask for bread. Don't write me those little hateful enforced scraps—written that I may not look in vain for the post in the morning. I am not a doll or a plaything but a passionate loving woman—& kindness will only choke me or kill me. If I have been wicked or done wrong, for God's sake don't let the punishment come by your hand. I love the truth but one lie I had rather believe in, is that there can be happiness even here below . . . Don't think when I write like this that it is in a fit of low spirits. I am well & strong today & have had a pleasant morning, & enjoyed myself greatly last night. These thoughts are always coming up within me. I try & I think our love is ideal & perfect & that your letters are all my heart longs for, & that they satisfy its uttermost cravings & when I see others love—I say to myself, mine is better, greater, purer, nobler—& the voice I cannot silence rises within me & says—"it is false". Oh! Darling I put my arms around you & kiss you with my kisses & say God bless you daily for joy far outweighs the misery—but . . . if we had drunk the cup out, let us put it down steadily—firmly—don't let us embitter the recollection of those sunny days. Oh! My tender love—write to me—don't be angry with me. I must write & tell you all I feel my own darling—because you alone can satisfy or soothe me. God bless & keep you darling—don't let me sadden your life. If any other women who love you can make you happier than I—then darling do not fear to leave me. I miss you darling.

Letter #2

Dearest Arthur,

I am unhappy at thinking you should be tempted to be not good. I cannot bear that you should ever be with anyone who is not nice or that it could be said he is just like other men. Oh Darling, don't touch pitch, don't even look at it. Put away from you what is unlovely & do not desecrate the sacred & beautiful expression of love. You owe it to your future wife during this time of probation to strive to become a man she may trust in & look up to. We come to you so pure & chaste. Why should you think it of little moment that the life of those we call our lord & master should bear so little daylight? I can a little forgive it where the man's affections are free & where he likes to amuse himself but you have your love & your little woman to fill up the blank. When we have a love we carry him in our hearts & he keeps us strong & faithful. Why is it not so with you? I can offer not the slightest reward for good behaviour because you have taken as your right the only thing I have to give but I can try to be even more tender & loving & pray that he may be kept from temptation & made strong & good. Good night. God bless you.

Your own devoted
Little Woman

One little question.

Oo does not kiss any but oo's own little woman does oo? Oh don't, it would hurt so. I could even bear never to be touched by you again if it were so. It is sad even to think that is a temptation to you.

Letter #3

My Dearest Arthur,

Chenny begs me tell you that she would like the tickets for "Caste" for Friday. We went to see it the other night & were quite charmed. It is quite idyllic. From my writing I suppose that there are not even to be any letters till October which is sad. I won't say what I think about it all because there must be no third person in matters of life & death that concern two. Still I feel strongly that if there is the slightest doubt about the love, it had better not be. Because to give up your family, the other love must almost be a blind passion. I say this with tears in my eyes & bitter sorrow in my heart for you yourself could not have wished for it more than I have, as being best & happiest for you both. In this world there is much tribulation but if there is a God who guides the events of this world I pray that he may still let it be, as being the best for both. You must not dream that I am less fond of you than in the days gone by. Not less! Oh no! Only you know one's heart & soul grow by intercourse. The feelings are all there warm & true, only so tight, so tight. May God bless & protect you from pain ever in darkness & sunshine.

Your truly loving
Louise Scott Russell

Rachel Russell broke off the engagement. Never married, Arthur's high living took its toll on his last years. Addicted to morphine, and an inveterate gambler, he was also an enormous spendthrift. His partner,

W. S. Gilbert, once noted, "My cook gets eighty pounds a year and gives me kipper. Sullivan's cook gets five hundred pounds a year for giving him the same thing in French." Arthur died at age fifty-eight without any of his close friends in attendance; W. S. Gilbert read the obituary in a paper while vacationing on the Continent.

Elizabeth I to Thomas Seymour

"My Lorde you need not to sende an excuse to me . . ."

Elizabeth I (1533–1603). Queen of England. The daughter of Henry VIII and his second wife, Anne Boleyn, the three-year-old's birth was declared illegitimate after the death of Henry's former wife, Catherine of Aragon. Catherine Parr, Henry VIII's sixth wife, became Elizabeth's primary caretaker, and, after Henry's death in 1547, Parr married the recipient of this letter, Lord High Admiral Thomas Seymour (1508–1549), the brother of Henry's third wife, Jane Seymour. This letter from the fifteen-year-old princess was a response to a note from Thomas written at the behest of his wife, who was outraged at her husband's flirtatious behavior toward the much younger Elizabeth. After catching the two in an embrace, she dismissed

THE 50 GREATEST LOVE LETTERS OF ALL TIME

Elizabeth from her residence at Hatfield, but permitted a correspondence with her husband to continue.

In 1549, Elizabeth was interrogated about a possible affair with Thomas and plotting to dethrone her stepbrother, King Edward VI. Thomas was executed for treason, and in 1553, upon Edward's death and the accession of Elizabeth's sister Mary, (a religious zealot intent on returning England to the Roman Catholic faith), Elizabeth was once again accused of conspiracy to overthrow the government. She was imprisoned in the Tower of London in 1554, and narrowly escaped execution.

Mary's popularity waned with her continuing childlessness and controversial marriage to Philip II, the ardently Catholic King of Spain. A disastrous war with France, the loss of Calais, and the burning of Protestants further eroded her popularity. Thus, Elizabeth's accession to the throne upon Mary's death on November 17, 1558, was welcomed with almost universal celebration.

My Lorde you neded not to sende an excuse to me, for I coulde not mistruste the not fulfillinge of your promes to prosede for want of good wyl, but only the oportunite serveth not, wherefore I shal desier you to thinke that a greater matter than this coulde not make me impute any unkindenis in you for I am a frende not wone with trifels . . . I comit you and al your affaires in Gods hande who kepe you from al evil . . .

"...a greater matter than this coulde not make me impute any unkindenis in you for I am a frende not wone with trifels..."

Henry VIII to Anne Boleyn

"... struck by the dart of love ..."

Henry VIII (1491–1547). King of England. One of the titanic figures of history, Henry had six wives: Catherine of Aragon (divorced; mother of Mary Tudor, known as "Bloody Mary"); Anne Boleyn (beheaded; mother of Elizabeth I); Jane Seymour (died twelve days after giving birth to Henry's successor, Edward VI); Anne of Cleves (divorced); Catherine Howard (beheaded); and Catherine Parr, who survived the King. Although he bore the papal title "Fidei Defensor" ("Defender of the Faith"), his relationship with the Vatican collapsed as a result of his desire to divorce Catherine of Aragon. His secret marriage to Anne Boleyn in 1533 further exacerbated his ties with the Roman Catholic Church and prompted him to establish the Church of England (Anglican Church), which invalidated his marriage to Catherine in 1534. This letter was written to Anne Boleyn before their marriage.

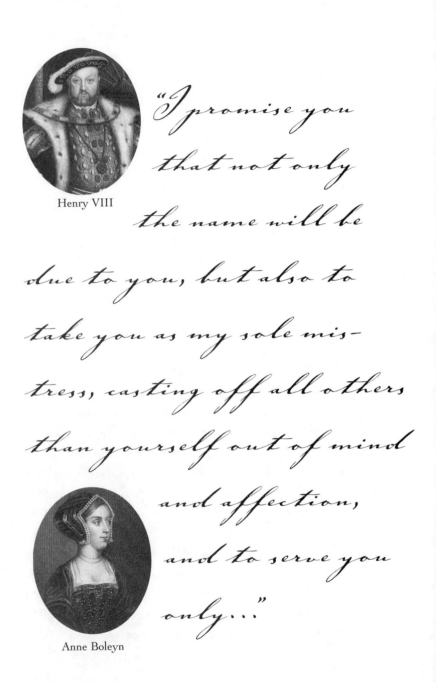

Henry VIII

Anne Boleyn

"I promise you that not only the name will be due to you, but also to take you as my sole mistress, casting off all others than yourself out of mind and affection, and to serve you only..."

In debating with myself the contents of your letters I have been put to a great agony; not knowing how to understand them, whether to my disadvantage as shown in some places, or to my advantage as in others. I beseech you now with all my heart definitely to let me know your whole mind as to the love between us; for necessity compels me to plague you for a reply. Having been for more than a year now struck by the dart of love, and being uncertain either of failure or of finding a place in your heart and affection, which point has certainly kept me for some time from naming you my mistress, since if you only love me with an ordinary love the name is not appropriate to you seeing that it stands for an uncommon position very remote from the ordinary; but if it pleases you to do the duty of a true, loyal mistress and friend, and to give yourself body and heart to me, who have been, and will be, your very loyal servant (if your rigour does not forbid me), I promise you that not only the name will be due to you, but also to take you as my sole mistress, casting off all others than yourself out of mind and affection, and to serve you only; begging you to make me a complete reply to this my rude letter as to how far and in what I can trust; and if it does not please you to reply in writing, to let me know of some place where I can have it by word of mouth, the which place I will seek out with all my heart. No more for fear of wearying you. Written by the hand of him who would willingly remain your

    H R

Within three months of his marriage to Anne, his ardor had cooled. Although she gave birth to the future Queen of England, Elizabeth I, Henry's primary goal was to have her produce a male heir. This was not to be. Anne was charged with adultery and incest with her brother and executed on May 19, 1536. Eleven days later, Henry wed Jane Seymour, who later bore him a son.

Charles Parnell to Katherine O' Shea

"I have been racked with torture
all today"

*Charles S. Parnell (1846–1891). Irish Nationalist leader, one of the
nineteenth century's most charismatic personalities. On October 13,
1881, Charles was imprisoned in Kilmainham (from whence this letter
was sent the following day) on charges stemming from his apparent
obstruction of Prime Minister Gladstone's Land Act. The letter's recipient, Katherine O'Shea, daughter of a reverend, was married to William
Henry O'Shea, an Irish politician (and supporter of Charles) who sat in
the British House of Commons. Katherine and Charles first met in 1880
and, after his release from prison (an initiative supported by her husband), she and Charles lived together in Eltham, outside London. There
she gave birth to three daughters by Charles. Though their relationship
was common knowledge, Katherine and her husband could not seek a*

Charles Parnell

divorce and risk offending her aunt, on whom they were financially dependent. The aunt's death in 1889 led to a battle between Katherine, the principal heir, and other relatives. Realizing that he would not share in the estate, William decided to separate from Katherine on the grounds of adultery, naming Charles as correspondent. The charges were not contested, and the divorce was granted, but the ensuing scandal cost Charles his political leadership and support. He married Katherine O'Shea in June 1891, four months before his untimely death at age forty-five.

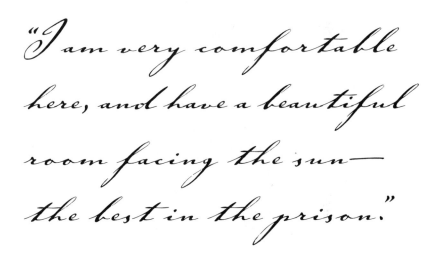

"I am very comfortable here, and have a beautiful room facing the sun — the best in the prison."

Kilmainham,
October 14, 1881.

My Own Dearest Wifie,

I have found a means of communicating with you, and of your communicating in return.

Please put your letters into enclosed envelope, first putting them into an inner envelope, on the joining of which you can write your initials with a similar pencil to mine, and they will reach me all right. I am very comfortable here, and have a beautiful room facing the sun—the best in the prison. There are three or four of the best of the men in adjoining rooms with whom I can associate all day long, so that time does not hang heavy nor do I feel lonely. My only fear is about my darling Queenie. I have been racked with torture all today, last night, and yesterday, lest the shock may have hurt you or our child. Oh, darling, write or wire me as soon as you get this that you are well and will try not to be unhappy until you see your husband again. You may wire me here.

I have your beautiful face with me here; it is such a comfort. I kiss it every morning.

Your King

Lewis Carroll to
Clara H. Cunnynghame

"Oh Hallie shy and still!"

Lewis Carroll (1832–1898). Pseudonym of Charles Lutwidge Dodgson, the English writer, logician, mathematician, photographer, and novelist; author of the classic Alice's Adventures in Wonderland *(1865), and its sequel,* Through the Looking-Glass *(1872). Carroll's most important relationships were those he formed with young girls, and the nature of these friendships has given rise to endless speculation about Carroll's sexual preferences, passions, proclivities, and possible perversions. These were not closed-door liaisons, however—Carroll was extremely proper about corresponding with his young friends, and always sought parental permission and involvement, especially when taking pictures of children posed in the nude. His letters are light-hearted, whimsical, and full of fun. The photographs more closely evoked Romantic idylls and were rarely provocative.*

Nevertheless, he always made sure that another adult, preferably a parent, was present during the studio sessions, and he rarely showed anyone the printed results. Prior to his death, Carroll destroyed most of the negatives and prints he had made of naked children. It is ironic that these images were taken during the height of the Victorian Age; if Carroll were alive and photographing today, he would have risked prosecution. His acquaintance with sixteen-year-old Clara Cunnynghame, the recipient of this poem, dates from January 1868, when he stayed at Croft Rectory and visited her family at their home in Ripon.

To "Hallie"
Oh Caledonian Maiden!
    Oh Hallie shy and still!
When'ere I hear sweet music,
    Of you my thoughts will fill.

I shall think of those "half hours"
    In Ripon spent with you;
I shall dream of great Beethoven
    And of Mendelssohn so true.

If "sleepless nights" assail me,
    And I toss about in vain,
The memory of Heller
    Will make me rest again.

A chord of "Caller Herrin;"
    A note of "Home Sweet Home;"
A bar of Scotland's "Blue Bells;"
    Will make my spirit roam

To a Drawing-room in the Crescent
Where those sweet sounds I heard,
And where I fain would follow
If I were <u>but</u> a bird.

Then Hallie! dear Childe Hallie!
Be to your "talent" true;
And sometimes when you're playing
Think <u>I</u> am watching you. —

Think how I <u>loved</u> your Music,
Nor for itself <u>alone</u>,
But for the <u>hands</u> that played it
The <u>mind</u> that felt its tone.

And now farewell "Childe Hallie"!
Though <u>I</u> am growing old,
Fond Mem'ry still will charm me,
To <u>you</u> I'll ne'er grow old.

Permissions

Letter from Virginia Woolf to Vita Sackville-West. Reprinted from *The Letters of Virginia Woolf, Vol III: 1923–1927*, by permission of Harcourt, Inc. Copyright © 1977 by Quentin Bell and Angelica Garnett.

Letter from Jack Kerouac to Sebastian Sampas. Reprinted by permission of Sterling Lord Literistic, Inc. Copyright © 1995 by John Sampas, Literary Rep.

Letter from Marjorie Fossa to Elvis Presley. Reprinted from *Letters to Elvis* by P. K. Mclemore, by permission of St. Martin's Press, LLC. Copyright © 1997 by P. K. Lemore.

Letter from Katherine Mansfield to John Middleton Murry. Reprinted from *Letters Between Katherine Mansfield and John Middleton Murry*, edited by Cherry A. Hankin, by permission of Ivan R. Dee, Publisher. Copyright © 1988 by The Estates of Katherine Mansfield and John Middleton Murry.

Letter from Oscar Wilde to Constance Wilde. Original letter courtesy of The Pierpont Morgan Library.

Letter from Frida Kahlo to Diego Rivera. Reprinted from *The Dairy of Frida Kahlo: An Intimate Self Portrait*, introduction by Carlos Fuentes, essay by Sarah M. Lowe. Copyright © 1995 by Harry N. Abrams Inc., New York. All rights reserved.

Letter from Emma Goldman to Ben Reitman. Reprinted from *Love, Anarchy, and Emma Goldman: A Biography*, edited by Candace Falk. Copyright © 1984, 1990 by Candace Falk.

Acknowledgments

I would very much like to thank Byron Preiss who first suggested the idea for this book, my editor Dinah Dunn and her associate Kelly Smith for their patience and perseverance, Rachel Kahan from Crown, Christine Nelson from the Pierpont-Morgan Library in New York, and Heather Wightman my personal assistant.

D.H.L.

David H. Lowenherz is president of Lion Heart Autographs, Inc., and has been a dealer in autographs and manuscripts since 1978. He is a member of the Grolier Club, a Fellow of the Morgan Library, and a co-founder and first president of the Professional Autograph Dealer's Association (PADA). Among his many appraisals were the papers of Irving Berlin, Abe Burrows, and Leonard Bernstein. His chief collecting interest is Robert Frost letters and inscribed first editions. He lives in New York with his wife, Nancy, and their four-year-old son, Jacob.